"ABBA:
The Making of an Unstoppable Musical Phenomenon"

Michael Mascioni

TABLE OF CONTENT

Chapter 1

Foreword

This book focuses largely on key milestones in ABBA's career, its cultural impact, the building of its "brand," and multimedia and interactive extensions of ABBA's music, which have helped sustain and extend its career. It isn't intended to provide an exhaustive review of ABBA's music and history. I've written the book as a longtime band fan and as a writer on music and multimedia experiences in museums and other leisure facilities.

This book is designed to provide a more multifaceted look at the band, explore its cultural roots, and examine the use of new technology to propel ABBA long into the future. The band's beginnings couldn't possibly foretell their stupendous success worldwide. They were pioneers at a time when Swedish pop groups had little impact globally. But they had cohesion and cadence that instantly captivated audiences—there was also the symmetry of two couples performing together and the colorful costumes, helping to create fantasies.

Chapter 2

ABBA's Indelible Impact on Pop Music Culture

What or who is ABBA?

ABBA, of course, is the legendary musical group with unrivaled worldwide success. ABBA's global impact has been staggering. According to figures from Pophouse Entertainment, the band has sold almost 400 million albums worldwide, produced 17 number-one hits, and generated more than 16 million weekly global streams. ABBA is reportedly the second most popular band in the world, behind the Beatles.

But the ABBA phenomenon transcends music and defies any sense of gravity. It triggers an infectious mood, a fantasy world, and a dream-like feeling that has universal appeal. ABBA is like a magical happiness pill, sending audiences into delirium. It's an unstoppable phenomenon that continues to soar like a rocket despite an unusually long hiatus when the group didn't record or perform together.

ABBA is also an atmosphere or environment that lends itself to multimedia and interactive productions and experiences. Its music is suffused with vivid, wondrous, and idealized motifs, such as the Dancing Queen.

My ABBA experience started in early 1974 when I first heard "Waterloo" blaring from a radio in my London hotel room, and I was immediately enchanted. I wondered who this magical band was and was enraptured by the almost quasi-dance hall sound and the music's infectious cadence.

I only saw the band perform live once a long time ago, but I have seen many performances of top-flight tribute bands, such as Arrival, and the sense of unbridled joy and wonderment is palpable from the very start of their shows.

Bjorn Ulvaeus calls "the whole story of ABBA a Cinderella story. An important ingredient is our amazing story—that we came to form a group in a natural way. Benny and I met and started working together. Quite apart from this fact, we got together with two women who happen to be great singers, a blonde and a redhead, who are also beautiful. We hung out, sang for the fun of it, and had no intention to start a group. Eventually, it became apparent that we should really do something together. It happened to be so genuine and organic that it is hard to put a finger on."

Then there was Stig Anderson and his breadth of knowledge and indomitable will to create something great outside Sweden. He convinced us to think, "Why not?" We saw that the only way to reach outside Sweden was the Eurovision Song Contest. Otherwise, the route was blocked. The Anglo-Saxon world was not listening to anything that came from here. It went directly into the trash. After "Waterloo," it did not go so well, and there were moments when I thought, "There's nothing other than this."

But the tide turned in their favor again after the release of the song "S.O.S." and a promotional video of the song in Australia. Ulvaeus highlights this turning point: Then it all took off with a bang. The British realized that there was life in that Eurovision group that should have died off long ago. We took off. It seems that many of our songs have become part of contemporary life. They are there all the time.

Ulvaeus pinpoints diverse factors responsible for the group's resilience and popularity over time with cross-generation groups: "I think one factor must be how we've sustained the song catalog through the years by, for example, Mamma Mia! the musical and the movies.

And then the songs themselves. We made such an impact in the '70s that there are people who've grown up with our music and carry that with them, playing it so that kids listen to it. And, for some reason, kids like our music. I've heard that a lot. Before we released Voyage, I think our songs had never been played more than they are now, and it's so global. Every country you go to, they know these songs. They don't necessarily know ABBA as such, but they know the songs.

I guess it also has to do with the sound of Agnetha and Frida. It's a unique sound. And it's totally by chance—we just happened to meet these women who were fantastic singers, and we started a group eventually. Agnetha is a soprano, and Frida is a mezzo, and when Frida meets Agnetha up there, there's a metallic, typical sound, which I can hear miles away.

There's also a particular kind of joyous, jubilant quality to the sound, which is very interesting because the lyrics are sad, and the songs might be in a minor key, but they still sound uplifting in some strange way. The music has Nordic roots, which might be exotic to the rest of the world, but not too exotic, and defines the songs amongst predominantly Anglo Saxon music."

Interestingly, the ABBA name developed inevitably, despite Ulvaeus's concern that "it was such a stupid name. And it is... I thought we should have a cool name like the Rolling Stones or something like that. The Northern Lights was one of our thoughts—and here we are with ABBA. We didn't have a choice in the matter. As we were kind of famous in Sweden, we made our first records under Agnetha, Benny, Bjorn, and Anni-Frid. The DJs on the radio got tired of saying that— 'Agnetha, Benny, Bjorn, and Anni-Frid'—as you can imagine. And so, they just abbreviated it to the initials ABBA."

Kenneth Partridge alludes to an otherworldly quality of ABBA: "It helped that the group was comprised of two married couples in satin costumes who lived on their own little island in Stockholm. ABBA was practically a fairytale." The band had a certain mystique.

A little-known fact about ABBA was that they needed permission to use the name in Sweden since a Swedish fish factory already used it. As Agnetha Fältskog explains, "We had to ask permission, and the factory said, 'OK, as long as you don't make us feel ashamed for what you're doing.' I think we did a good job."

ABBA has effectively spawned an industry around the band. Indeed, ABBA can be called a "brand," one that has been cultivated over time via multiple media. The brand is as instantly recognizable as a brand like Coke. Professor Nigel Nicholson, the evolutionary psychologist at the London Business School, echoes this point, saying, "ABBA has always been a brand and was always a business at heart. All successful bands intersect with the culture using sound, appearance, and an ethos that people can instantly relate to."

A central element of ABBA's brand was its iconic logo, which came from the mind of designer Rune Söderqvist. The official ABBA site explains his approach to accentuating the symmetrical factor in the logo: "Rune's thinking was that each 'B' (Bjorn and Benny) should be turned towards each 'A' (Agnetha and Anni-Frid) since they were two couples." As such, with this creation,

Söderqvist cemented the mirrored design element into ABBA's visuals and continued to integrate symmetry into the rest of the album covers, which he went on to create.

The marketing element in ABBA generated a firestorm of criticism in some quarters, especially earlier in ABBA's career, but the band was unfazed by this criticism. Stig Anderson, the band's former manager and co-founder of Polar Music, responded to that criticism this way: "If you're writing good songs, why shouldn't the marketing be as good as the rest of it? After all, this is the first time in the history of show business that there has been 100% artistic control of the writing, marketing, recording, and record label. We're not just giving it to some third, fourth, fifth, or sixth party."

ABBA's sound is natural, organic, and well-crafted, not manufactured.

Bjorn Ulvaeus sarcastically scoffed at charges by some that ABBA's music and act were formulaic: "Yes, we had a formula, a hit factory! And we were two couples who married each other as a gimmick. All those things we were accused of. But the claims have no basis other than in their own absurdity. If you listen to the songs today, they are so different from each other. We tested all sorts of styles, not knowing what it was that made people like it. It was hurtful to hear that we did the songs based on anything other than pure speculation."

Per Sundin, CEO at Pophouse Entertainment, stresses the key role of branding and cross-promotion in ABBA's long-term success: "ABBA is a perfect example of how to treat a catalog. They did their last album in 1981 (prior to 2021). Fast forward to 2020, and they made more money from their music 40 years later approximately. And that's very interesting, because (it shows) what the Mamma Mia! musical did. One of the big reasons (why ABBA's music made more money in 2020 than 1981) is that the music is fantastic... what Bjorn and Benny created, together with Frida and Agnetha's voices, is just unbelievably good. But (the other reason) is that music ages better than wine, better than anything. It's like real estate property. So (ABBA 's) constantly evolving, keeping the music alive, keeping that fantastic music exposed to new generations. That's really a stellar phenomenon."

The band has tightly and carefully controlled its legacy and forged an alternative career path and multimedia brand in an organic way, building up successive brand layers. This has involved the co-creation or outsourcing of diverse multimedia experiences and environments relating to their music, including the Mamma Mia! musical and films, the ABBA Voyage show, ABBA The Museum, and the Mamma Mia! interactive parties. Ingmarie Halling, Creative Director and Curator of ABBA The Museum, stresses the band's involvement in so many creative and business decisions: "They were 100% involved in every decision, from costumes, songs, tours, tickets... everything. If one disapproved of something, it didn't happen."

ABBA's willingness to experiment, such as its collaboration on the ABBA Voyage show, has ensured its longevity and appeal with new as well as old fans.

ABBA also had the mystique of a band seemingly emerging from a territory not well known for rock/pop music at the time they entered the scene. The fact that their musical experience was continually refreshed and enhanced over the years through musicals, films, and multimedia productions clearly has extended the lifespan of their music. Most importantly, the band has had close involvement with many of these properties. They co-produced, shepherded, financed, and had some control over many of them, lending their imprimatur and authenticity to the spinoffs.

Bjorn Ulvaeus alludes to the band's judicious cultivation of its music, especially relating to films: "We have been very, very careful about what we've done. We've never allowed our music in commercials, for instance, and we've basically just been doing things that we think, 'yeah, this is high quality, this is high cred,' and nothing else. They send us a whole script, and we tell them to send a synopsis or a whole script—and every time, we know immediately when it's a good one. But we say no to at least 90% of the ones we get."

Ulvaeus has played a strong role in ABBA-related and non-ABBA-related ventures beyond the Mamma Mia! musical. He is part co-founder and owner of Pophouse Entertainment, a multimedia entertainment company whose properties include the gaming center Space in Stockholm. A notable development was Pophouse's recent purchase of Kiss's music catalog. Ulvaeus is also President of CISAC, the global federation of authors' societies and the largest network of creators worldwide.

Madison Kim proclaims that "ABBA's revolutionary impact on the world is undeniable, with aspects of their music found in every crevice of culture today. Their signature sound has served as a blueprint for several prominent producers in the pop scene today. ABBA's orchestral elements inspired Max Martin and has stated how he 'ripped off' their discography to write the 'perfect pop song.'"

Nate Sloan, assistant professor of musicology at the University of Southern California, believes the blending of ABBA's two (female) singers was key to their sound: "If the two vocalists are singing the same note, it adds this really cool color to have their different vocals, giving each their own interpretation." He also feels their "maximalist pop" sound was central to their success and vitality: "There is so much happening in ABBA songs. Their music is very orchestral. 'Mamma Mia' is a great example of this. You hear a marimba at the very beginning of the song, but then you have synthesizers. It's this mix of traditional, orchestral, symphonic, and then very new synthesis, electronic."

Warrick Thompson, a classical and opera journalist, also calls attention to the mélange of musical styles exhibited in ABBA's music: "Key to Bjorn and Benny's originality is their readiness to draw from different and even unlikely musical genres, such as oom-pah German Schlager ('I Had a Dream'), church chorale ('Lay All Your Love'), rock ('On and On and On'), tango ('Head Over Heels'), balladry ('Thank You for the Music'), Scottish folk ('Arrival'), disco ('Dancing Queen'), prog rock ('The Visitors'), and so on."

But they were never slavish imitators. In each case, they took what they wanted from the tropes of each genre and turned them into something fresh. The critic Ivan Hewitt suggests that this deracination has contributed to ABBA's longevity. He wrote that as time passes, the songs' profusion of vague floating cultural signifiers becomes more and more advantageous. It allows every generation to find its own emotional life mirrored in them.

Another factor that made ABBA sound like ABBA is the sheer beauty of its textures. The group loved the "wall of sound" principle pioneered by Phil Spector, and their studio engineer, Michael Tretow, created a double-tracked studio sound to ensure that the band sounded both polished and huge. And the orchestrations are adorable. Don't the flutes and drums in 'Fernando' immediately conjure up a military campfire under a starry Mexican night sky? Doesn't the repetitive falling synth riff in the introduction to "The Day Before You Came" create a world of banality, ready to be overturned by love? Then there's the blending of the husky sound of Frida and the lighter timbre of Agnetha, both of whose voices blossom under the microphone.

Such memorable perfection makes adapting or arranging the songs for other media all trickier. This is why there are very few successful cover versions of ABBA songs, and the ones that work best retain much of the original ABBA sound. Erasure got it right, as did Sinéad. But for every success, there are a hundred fails, such as the oh-so-hilarious New Zealand rock album "ABBA Salutely" or the appalling orchestral inflations of the RPO or the LSO "Playing ABBA."

Judy Craymer, producer of the Mamma Mia! musical and films, believed that "there are two generations of ABBA songs that take you through their journey—the younger and poppy songs from the beginning of the ABBA period, and then the more emotional songs, the big power ballads, dramas like The Winner Takes It All and Knowing Me, Knowing You. I would say Dancing Queen is one of the most brilliant songs ever, but I would also say The Winner Takes It All is a ballad that musically and lyrically is a landscape of emotions."

Daniel Levitin, a musician and former producer, added: "The way ABBA's songs are performed and produced, apart from the underlying composition, gives them an overall catchy sound." In his book The World in Six Songs: How the Musical Brain Created Human Nature, Levitin explores how evolutionary biology influences musical tastes. He argues: "If you look at the evolutionary biology of the species and the chemical reactions we have to events in the world, for tens of thousands of years when we as a species heard music, we heard groups singing it, not an individual and not an individual standing on a stage. So, the ABBA model of the multiple voices or the Edwin Hawkins singers singing Oh Happy Day is much closer to stimulating these evolutionary echoes of what music really is, fundamentally—closer than, say, Frank Sinatra or Miley Cyrus."

ABBA benefited from the law of scarcity. The band's long absence from new recordings and live performances significantly increased demand. Their return with the Voyage album in 2021 after a 40-year gap was remarkable. Jadeep Varma highlighted this: "No entity in the history of music ever made a comeback after 40 years."

ABBA's alternative career path, especially through multimedia and technology, has broad implications for today's music industry. They've resisted the conventional route of simply becoming a jukebox machine. Instead, they've pioneered a template for artists seeking to expand their creative and entertainment ambitions beyond standard parameters.

Another factor that contributed to ABBA's enduring appeal was their non-controversial, happy music, which resonated especially during times of political and social upheaval. Sarah Wiggins observed: "ABBA's popularity has surged during times of political and social turmoil. Waterloo won the Eurovision Song Contest in 1974 when the UK was grappling with inflation, strikes, the oil embargo crisis, and ongoing conflict in Northern Ireland. Similarly, the US was dealing with the aftermath of the Vietnam War and the Watergate scandal. Waterloo rose towards the top of the charts in both countries, reaching #1 in the UK and #6 in the US. A similar phenomenon occurred in 2008 with the release of the first Mamma Mia! movie, which premiered during the Great Recession. Despite mixed critical reviews, the film grossed $600 million worldwide on a budget of $62 million, becoming the fifth-highest-grossing musical movie of all time."

Extensive audience participation has been central to the ABBA music experience, and the interactive properties relating to ABBA have effectively exploited that element. ABBA's long-term success has also been due to its cross-generational appeal, which has sustained and boosted their visibility and popularity over time.

ABBA's career can be viewed through the prism of key progressions or seasons of life. They started out on a smaller level but leaped to a higher level after winning the 1974 Eurovision Contest, reached even higher levels of success afterward, retired from recording and performing ABBA music after a relatively short time, reemerged in the spotlight with the ABBA Gold albums and the Mamma Mia! musicals and films, enjoyed renewed popularity with the Voyage album and multimedia show, and were just recently knighted by Sweden's king and queen.

ABBA paved the way for other Swedish rock/pop groups, such as Roxette. Carl Magnus Palm, a historian and writer about ABBA, echoes this point: "I think ABBA's main contribution in that regard is that they showed it could be done. Despite being from Sweden, largely regarded as a pop/rock backwater back then, ABBA managed to sustain a career beyond one or two hits. In terms of the international music business, ABBA's success opened the eyes of the international music business to the fact that pop music can come from anywhere yet appeal to everyone.

And, in terms of the Swedish music business, the impossible dream must have seemed a lot less impossible. Instead of thinking, 'Well, we're from Sweden, it could never happen,' maybe they thought, 'Well, we're from Sweden, so we have that against us, but ABBA managed an international career, so...'"

Mike Watson, who played bass on most records for ABBA from 1972–1982 and its previous incarnation as the Party People (Folkfest) band from 1970–1971, has distinct recollections of the band's impact from the beginning. (He also played on a single for Anni-Frid Lyngstad in 1972 and appeared as Napoleon on the cover of ABBA's Waterloo album but didn't tour with the band.) He attributes ABBA's strong appeal largely to several factors: "the unique way the voices of Agnetha Fältskog and Lyngstad came together, the band's great songwriting, the band's 'clean' image (as the band didn't do drugs or drink and wasn't plagued by scandal), and the band's appeal to a wide cross-section of people."

Although he believes interest in ABBA's music remained high even after the band disbanded, he regards the Mamma Mia! musicals in the 1990s and the re-release of Arrival in the mid-1990s as a kind of major "comeback for the band" commercially. Watson feels "ABBA was really the first Swedish rock/pop group to enjoy worldwide success," though he notes "Blue Suede had a rock hit worldwide earlier." He adds, "ABBA paved the way for the success of Swedish bands like Roxette and Max Martin."

Carl Magnus Palm, a celebrated writer and historian on ABBA, offers intriguing insights into making ABBA's music in his book ABBA – The Complete Recording Sessions, about how ABBA wrote and recorded their music. He published a companion volume to that book called ABBA – On Record in March, which focused on what happened to the music after the recordings and included stories of how the album sleeves were put together and how record companies promoted ABBA.

Although Palm believes it's hard to quantify ABBA's appeal. he asserts that "they had a lot of great songs that appealed to a lot of people." In his view, the band's music is very energetic, happy, accessible, and has cross-generational appeal. The band didn't pretend their music was important art, although their lyrics had meaning if you looked for it. He notes that the band's records were still selling quite well, in the hundreds of thousands well into the 1980s, but hadn't reached the level of a legacy act yet at the time.

In Palm's view, "the fact that the band never came back and didn't have a reunion until very recently for the Voyage album let the music speak for itself and created tension. With the introduction of the Mamma Mia! musicals interactive party and the Voyage show, the band showed that there were other ways to consume their music and demonstrated that they had become a franchise."

In fact, Palm believes the quality of ABBA's music was and still is seriously underestimated by many people. In his view, their music boasts considerable craftsmanship and is more difficult to play than many expect.

Towards the end of the band's main career in 1981-82, certain attitudes towards the band changed. They were taken more seriously and received more respect, though the media were still critical of what they perceived as their business attitude. ABBA's image was enhanced considerably by the release of the ABBA Gold compilation album in 1992, and they were taken even more seriously. Today, ABBA's image is very different. Now, they're legends. People recognize the emotional resonance of their music. The difference between their early period and the period starting in the early 1990s is like night and day. People obviously missed ABBA's music, and their revival never subsided.

As Palm mentions, one of the most amazing aspects of the band's revival success from the 1990s onward is that they enjoyed great popularity without touring, unlike most other bands. They found different ways to funnel their music— through the Mamma Mia! musicals, the Voyage show, and the interactive Mamma Mia! restaurant parties, and they all succeeded, he points out. One of the band's advantages in this regard is that their music was already in party mode and conveys a feeling of happiness and letting loose, he stresses. As a result, they were able to exploit these new properties in a way that wouldn't be possible with bands like The Beatles, he maintains. Based on these efforts, "ABBA essentially extended their brand, made the brand stronger, and kept the music alive," Palm believes.

Another factor that probably influenced the band to expand into other ventures relating to their music is that "a number of ABBA tribute bands appeared on the scene and profited from the ABBA brand, but ABBA itself didn't benefit from shows of those bands other than receiving royalties," according to him.

Palm doesn't believe there will ever be another ABBA. In his view, "They arrived at a time when the music business worked in a different way. ABBA's talents and skills were particular to that time."

Helga van de Kar, President of the Official ABBA International Fan Club, thinks "ABBA's music is timeless and has magic. Benny is a real genius with the music, and Bjorn is the same with the lyrics. I feel their music and lyrics grew over time. And perhaps it's because Benny and Bjorn don't read music and don't record all the time. They always did it by memory. So if they came up with a good melody, it came back to them, and they remembered it. Benny is still playing the piano every day."

All of us at the Official International ABBA Fan Club think the music from the Voyage album is fantastic. Parts of the music on that album could be from the 70s, and some of the songs sound really new. In some of the songs, the voices of Agnetha and Anni-Frid sound lower because of their age. The ABBA Voyage concert is spectacular—an event that's never been done before. ABBA won't do something unless they're sure of it. They want everything to be perfect. "I Still Have Faith in You" is a fantastic song. It's a new ABBA song and covers their past. You can hear that Benny has grown musically.

Janne Schaffer had an interesting entrée into ABBA 's musical projects. He first met Benny Andersson and Bjorn Ulvaeus when he worked as a session guitarist at Polar Studios in 1971. He was asked by the two to play guitar on the debut album of a 15-year-old musician called Ted Gardestad, who enjoyed great popularity in Sweden. Both Agnetha Faltskog and Anni-Frid Lyngstad sang on that record. In 1972, he was asked to play on the song 'People Need Love' on an album for Folkfest, the original name for ABBA. He recorded with ABBA again in 1973. On all of these records, Schaffer played with a team of session musicians, including Mike Watson, and compared the team to the Wrecking Crew. He remembered that period as an intense period. Interestingly, my solo album in 1973 sold more than ABBA's records at the time, according to him. Schaffer also added some musical ideas to the Waterloo album and then proceeded to go on tour with Shawn Phillips in the US in 1974. When he returned to Sweden that year, he was asked to join ABBA on tour but had to decline, as his son was one year old at the time, and he wanted to spend more time at home. Lasse Wellander then took his place on tour. Schaffer played on 46 ABBA songs and worked on ABBA records until 1981.

As Schaffer recalled, ABBA 's recording process started with musical ideas from Benny, who would start playing piano, then chords would be written, and arrangements were worked out. The supporting musicians would be asked for some musical ideas, and the ones that were accepted would be incorporated into the music. For example, Schaffer contributed a country-style guitar part to one song. He points out that "nothing was written" before the start of ABBA recordings.

Schaffer recalled that Benny and Bjorn were inspired by Phil Spector's wall of sound technique and utilized it to a great extent on the song "Ring Ring." In that song, the basic guitar parts were doubled. Benny and Bjorn asked me for a little Ring Ring sound in the refrain, and I changed the song's tuning on my own album from a low E to D. Schaffer appreciated being included in the arrangements of ABBA's songs. He believes that "he and other session musicians were hired because of our inventiveness," and ABBA liked my musical ideas. He adds that he's proud of the work I did with the band.

Schaffer said, "he had no idea ABBA would be so popular, and he doesn't have a complete explanation for it." But, at the same time, he said all the musicians in the ABBA recordings worked as hard as possible to make the tunes as good as possible. He also notes that "Benny and Bjorn took their time to record" and highlights "the high quality of the music." In that respect, he compares ABBA's painstaking, laborious approach to recording with that of bands like the Beatles and Queen. Overall, he attributes the band's success to their very good songs and the extremely good vocals of Agnetha and Anni-Frid. He adds that Agnetha's vocals are something special and feels she's one of the best vocalists around.

Schaffer occasionally plays in Europe with an ABBA tribute band called ABBA Mania.

Ola Johansson, Professor of Geography at the University of Pittsburgh/Johnstown, believes ABBA "served as a role model for other Swedish pop bands." According to him, "they helped build an infrastructure for Swedish pop music. ABBA showed that Swedish pop music could gain traction on an international level, and the band could serve as a trigger for Swedish pop music to be commercially successful and have some artistic value as well. In addition, some people in and around ABBA remained active in the Swedish music business even after the band disbanded, and the band, in effect, trained other Swedish pop musicians in the process of music making."

Johansson feels ABBA is different in a number of ways. In his view, their music "wasn't really rock or R&B. They were inspired by an earlier form of pop music in Sweden and Europe. Their music had a lighter touch and was more focused on vocal harmonies and less on the beat. They had simple melodies. The piano also played a big role in their music and greatly affected their songwriting. Essentially, ABBA merged the more European style of pop music with rock music."

Stany Van Wymeersch, author of such books on ABBA as The Legacy of ABBA, describes Bjorn Ulvaeus and Benny Andersson as "pop masters who write perfect pop music and write the classical music of the future. Benny and Bjorn are genius composers. Benny is like the Mozart or

Beethoven of our time." Van Wymeersch believes "there are so many ingredients in ABBA's music, and several sources influence their music you wouldn't ordinarily find in pop music. Agnetha brings schlager music, Bjorn brings folk music (Hootenanny Singers), Frida brings jazz standards, and Benny brings rock music (the Hep Stars) from their pre-ABBA careers to create a new, unique sound. Most of the songs are interpreted perfectly by Agnetha and Frida. They're excellent singers. The songs of Benny and Bjorn reached their pinnacle with Agnetha and Frida singing. Their other songs are of the same high quality, but don't have the same impact with other people singing." Van Wymeersch adds that Benny and Bjorn's musical approach was shaped by "listening closely to American, British, German, French, and Italian music on the Swedish radio. No music was excluded."

John Semley, writer for This is Pop - Stockholm Syndrome, feels that the major key to ABBA's success was "its great songs." He also believes that "ABBA's disbanding and disappearance from the pop music scene actually redounded to their benefit, and the band attracted new audiences. Over time, the band was rediscovered as the music landscape changed. Music fans became less cultish, and it became cool to like ABBA's music." In Semley's view, "ABBA was ahead of their time. They proved that pop bands could write their own music, and not just be a product of producers and Brill Building writers, for example." He contends "there hasn't been a band as massively influential as ABBA."

Dr. Jadey O'Regan, lecturer in Contemporary Music at the Sydney Conservatorium of Music, and co-author of Hooks in Music, believes the band often didn't receive credit for their accomplishments because they were unfashionable. According to her, "While many consider ABBA's music cheesy or uncool if you listen to the depths of their arrangements, their songs are very sophisticated— the layers, chords, melodies—are all cleverly put together to connect with so many people over such a long time. I am constantly amazed at the arrangement of a song like 'Dancing Queen,' which feels effortless, but is made up of endless catchy hooks."

Victoria Norback, the founder, show producer, and singer for the ABBA tribute band Arrival from Sweden, attributes ABBA's success to their very good songs and the fact that they were fantastic musicians and singers. The quality of their records was very high, and they used the latest recording techniques. She notes that they played "so many different types of songs, including songs as diverse as Fernando and Dancing Queen. They never copied themselves. In that sense, they were like the Beatles." She notes that ABBA integrates "a lot of Swedish folk music in its songs."

ABBA Mania was particularly pronounced in Australia early on. Annie Wright, former RCA Sydney Promotions Manager, recounts the group's huge impact in Australia: "I had no idea what lay before me. It was just an explosion. We knew they had perfect pop songs, but no one could have predicted the extent to which Australia would embrace them. It was nothing like I've ever experienced before or since. It was very surreal for everyone, from (promoter) Paul Dainty to the band themselves…Nothing has ever come close to the hysteria, the adoration. And most people never knew that Australia was where they broke. ABBA loved performing for Australians; they loved the reaction. It became a real family. Australians became their family."

The Countdown show in Australia played a key role in sparking ABBA's popularity there. On the show, host Ian Molly Meldrum played their music videos. He reports, "We got a great reaction from the public."

Ulvaeus also recalls the tremendous support ABBA received from Australia during their 1977 tour there: "The fantastic, amazing thing was having people along all that way, waving flags and banners. That was something incredible because that rarely happened those days, anywhere." In fact, Ulvaeus credits Australia for their "comeback" after the band "struggled" to retain their popularity with their follow-up song to "Waterloo."

ABBA's influence has extended to tribute albums centering around their music. As Madison Kim reports, the band's discography has spawned several tribute albums, ranging from Cher's Dancing Queen to the London Symphony Orchestra's ABBA Played by the London Symphony Orchestra.

ABBA: The Movie, a rockumentary film written and directed by Lasse Hallström, was shot during their 1977 Australian tour and remastered in 2008. It provided key insights into the ABBA phenomenon. It coincided with the release of ABBA: The Album and included songs ranging from the album to ABBA's earliest hits. The movie also featured previously unavailable songs, such as "Get on the Carousel." One critic called ABBA: The Movie "really the first widescreen pop music showcase… It remains a very rare portrait of a 70s pop band at the height of its popularity."

Ulvaeus had some initial reservations about the film: "…Quite honestly, I don't think that films with pop stars work very well. Of course, The Beatles are an exception, and Tommy was a big hit…but there have been lots of other pop films that have sunk without a trace… Seeing the film came as a bit of a shock. It's hard to recognize yourself up there on a giant screen in Panavision. But then we've had many moments when it has been hard to accept the things that have been happening to us."

Jared Raab, director of This is Pop - Stockholm Syndrome, attributes much of ABBA's success to "its great songs, incredibly catchy melodies that stick with you, and their energetic, timeless music. They always gave top performances." He says ABBA's music was influenced significantly by "the traditional dance band and schlager sound in Sweden." In his view, ABBA had "great self-confidence—they thought that if the Beatles could write their own songs and succeed, they could, too." He also believes "the idea of switching singers was inspired by the Beatles." In addition, he observes that every ABBA song was different, and they continued to expand their music. He derived some of his insights about the band from his interview with Benny Andersson on This is Pop - Stockholm Syndrome.

In his view, ABBA was highly successful at "reinventing themselves. They were already mounting massive multimedia spectacles before the Mamma Mia! musicals. For example, 'they made backdrops for their shows in fabric that could be rolled up or unrolled, depending on the size of their shows. That allowed them to more easily perform in all markets.' So, it wasn't a big leap from their original live shows to the production of the Voyage shows. They showed that their music could live on."

Phyllida Lloyd, director of the Mamma Mia! musical, attributes the strong impact of ABBA's music to "a combination of things. I think their music has genius melodies by Benny Andersson and really quite complex and intricate orchestration. They were sort of masters of studio production, and they used every gizmo in the book available at that time, including a very ornate use of vocal harmony and words used partly as orchestration."

Raab believes ABBA helped drive Swedish pop music forward in the sense that "they showed Swedish pop musicians following them that they could break through internationally. They set a benchmark for other Swedish pop musicians." In fact, he feels "Swedish pop music from artists like Max Martin changed the face of North American pop music in the 90s, as they worked with such top artists in the US and the UK as Britney Spears and the Backstreet Boys."

One of the most fascinating aspects of ABBA is its ability to regenerate its music and continually attract new audiences. Social media has brought ABBA a whole new generation of fans, as many younger fans have learned about the group through platforms like TikTok and

Facebook. As Gemma Ballam, a teenager from Moray, Scotland, said, "TikTok is making the band accessible to a new generation."

Finn Sjoberg, a guitarist who toured with ABBA from 1974 to 1977, recalls that the band played with a lot of energy and enjoyed working with the band. He feels the Voyage album has very good material and sounds like ABBA, but finds the Voyage concert in London very strange, as the live band plays exactly the same songs every night. Though he hasn't actually seen the show, he's heard good things about it from many people. He doesn't believe there will be another ABBA, largely because it took four talents that good to play music at the highest level. As he puts it, It's like with the Beatles. Can you imagine another Beatles?

ABBA endured some fallow times in their career, especially in the 80s and 90s. However, support from such groups as the gay community kept them afloat. Ulvaeus states, "In the 80s, ABBA was distinctly uncool. And I thought, 'Well, that's it. It was fun while it lasted, but now it's over.' But for some strange reason, we still remained popular on the gay scene. And—maybe it sounds like I'm sucking up, but I don't care—when we got a revival in the late 80s and early 90s, I'm sure it's because we stayed popular on the gay scene."

Alluding to ABBA's longevity, Warwick Thompson points out, "As keepers of the flame, Benny and Bjorn have astutely curated the group's heritage with musicals and museums." He underlines the triumphant return of ABBA to the studio— "after 40 long years, the band has finally caved into siren calls to reform. The group's manager, Gorel Hanser, was present at the recording sessions and commented, 'It was wonderful. It was like no time had passed at all. It was like in the olden days. They were happy; it was easy and warmhearted. There was magic in the music, in the studio, and in the song. It has ABBA's melancholy and their sound—but it's a modern ABBA song.'"

ABBA reached another important milestone when they were inducted into the Rock and Roll Hall of Fame in 2010 in New York, with Benny Andersson and Anni-Frid Lyngstad accepting the award for the group.

ABBA has also been a strong supporter of altruistic causes. The band gifted royalties from their song Chiquitita to UNICEF to assist child psychology and protection services in Guatemala. This helped raise $5 million for the program. Bjorn Ulvaeus is ecstatic about the results: "Never in my wildest dreams could I have expected that it would be so long-lasting and bring in so much money.

It's the best legacy anyone could wish for." ABBA also gave royalties in 2021 from their song Little Things to the same UNICEF protection program for children, aimed at helping girls affected by the COVID-19 pandemic.

Clearly, ABBA continues to be firmly rooted in pop music culture, and its multimedia properties continue to resonate, impact, and resilience today.

He describes the music for the musical Kristina as "a more classical kind of music."

Chapter 3

The Pivotal Role of ABBA's Victory at the 1974 Eurovision Contest in Their Worldwide Success

The pivotal role of ABBA winning the 1974 Eurovision Contest in Brighton, England, with the song "Waterloo" in their worldwide success can't be overstated. As Dr. Jadey O'Regan asserts, "'Waterloo' was ABBA's first worldwide hit. The song 'Ring Ring' had been a hit the year earlier in Europe; however, it was 'Waterloo' that introduced the world to ABBA's music. 'Waterloo' was specifically written for the Eurovision Song Contest, so it was a song built for purpose and success." She said, 'Waterloo's lyrics were oblique. They are referencing a historic battle as a metaphor for a relationship. I can't think of another song that does this. And the way the lyrics were delivered was also unique. ABBA has a particular way of pronouncing English that catches the ear and is part of their identifiable sound. The song had a shiny arrangement and it had definite elements of glam, but in a new kind of package, and with female singers."

She adds, "'Waterloo' set ABBA up for a string of unforgettable singles that are particularly loved here in Australia."

Referencing the critical role of Eurovision in ABBA's worldwide success, James Rogan flatly asserts that "ABBA are the ultimate pragmatists. It was a pragmatic decision to go into Eurovision because it was the only platform that could launch them into the Anglophone world of music at that level."

Stany Van Wymeersch concurs, saying, "The Eurovision Contest was the only international platform at the time that could introduce ABBA to a wider audience internationally. It provided their career with an enormous boost. The band was already highly successful in Sweden and some other European countries. For example, 'Ring Ring' was a number 1 single in Belgium."

The Beatles had a major influence on ABBA's creation of "Waterloo," as Bjorn Ulvaeus notes: "Our biggest inspiration was the Beatles. And we so much wanted to be that pop group. I think 'Waterloo' is in a tradition of pure pop and in the tradition of the fantastic music that was written around the end of the 50s, beginning of the 60s, in the Brill Building and Carole King and (Gerry) Goffin, and then the Beatles. So, the true pop songs, the really good pop songs, that's where we were coming from, and that's what we wanted to express with 'Waterloo.'"

The song reached the top of the charts in many European countries and hit the top 10 in Australia and the US, in addition to being a massive hit in Sweden.

Chapter 4

The ABBA Brand Strikes Gold with Mamma Mia! Musical and Films

Few extensions of ABBA's music, such as the musical Mamma Mia!, have propelled the band's brand as far as this one. It had a tremendous impact on extending ABBA's career after the band disbanded and exploited the audience participation aspect of their performances to a great degree. Reportedly, over 65 million people have seen Mamma Mia! in over 60 countries on 6 continents, raking in over $4 billion in revenue since the musical's opening in London's West End.

Ola Johansson believes ABBA's continued popularity is partly due to key extensions of their music, such as the Mia! Musicals and films. As he puts it, ABBA's music continues in another form, such as the Mamma Mia! musicals and films. They've been particularly successful in reviving ABBA's music because they're able to basically remake the music and are conducive to perpetuating the music.

According to John Semley, "The Mamma Mia! musicals helped to expand audiences for ABBA's music and propel their staying power. It made sense to come back the way they did."

The story for Mamma Mia!, which was developed by theater producer Judy Craymer, focuses on Donna, a single mother running a crumbling hotel in Greece; her spirited daughter Sophie who's about to get married; and the girl's three possible fathers, who pay them a visit. The girl conducts a search for her biological father after learning about three men her mother dated from her diaries. She intends for her real father to walk her down the aisle at her wedding.

It's not widely known that the making of the musical evolved through many iterations. Craymer presented the idea of a story based around ABBA's songs of love and loss" to Ulvaeus and Andersson a year after ABBA disbanded, but they were hesitant. (She first met Ulvaeus and

Andersson while working on the musical Chess.) As Ulvaeus explains, "She approached me with an idea to produce a standalone TV special with a story loosely based on ABBA songs. I don't know why that didn't work out, but now it was going to be a pantomime show. We looked at several scripts, but none of them really worked. But Judy didn't give up. After factoring in the collaboration of Ulvaeus and Andersson on the musical Chess, she switched her approach and raised the idea of a musical. She introduced me to dramatist Catherine Johnson, and now we were talking about a full-fledged musical. I had just seen a production of Grease with two of my kids, and I thought maybe this is what it could be—an uplifting rom-com musical with lots of hit songs. But could you really write a musical backward, that is, to weave a credible story around existing songs without changing the lyrics? Having met Catherine, I thought, if anyone can pull that off, she can."

On paper, Johnson wasn't a likely candidate for writer of the play, as she had never written a musical before and was known for her ability to capture intensity in drama. But Craymer saw her potential and commissioned Johnson to write the book for Mamma Mia! in 1997. By 1998, the narrative emerged. A young girl, Sophie, discovers her mother Donna's diaries in the lead-up to her own wedding. Through them, her burning curiosity about the identity of her own unidentified father is reignited, leading her to contact the three potential men revealed within the diary, inviting them to her mother's small Grecian inn with hopes that their reunion will somehow reveal her parentage. Hijinks ensue, and no biological father is revealed. But by the end of the piece, a five-pronged family has been formed.

The story, which plays on numerous classic tropes (including mistaken identity, the power of three, audience participation, and even a literal Greek chorus), had its director by 1998 when Phyllida Lloyd came on board. Then known as an opera director, her ability to mould and shape epic stories served her well with Mamma Mia! elevating the piece alongside Johnson to what felt like a modern fable before it had seen an audience.

The play debuted successfully in London at the Prince Edward Theatre in April 1999. It comprised "21 songs, including Super Trouper, Lay All Your Love on Me, Dancing Queen, Knowing Me, Knowing You, Thank You for the Music, Money, Money, Money, The Winner Takes It All, Voulez Vous, and Mamma Mia!, along with a sing-along reprise of Mamma Mia!, Dancing Queen, and Waterloo." Following the play's initial London run, the show opened at the Royal

Alexandra Theatre in Toronto in May 2000, running for five years. It played in San Francisco, Los Angeles, and Chicago before debuting in New York at the Winter Garden Theatre in October 2001. The play moved to the Broadhurst Theatre in New York in 2013. All in all, Mamma Mia! notched 5,758 performances on Broadway. Its 25th-anniversary national tour in the US recouped the $4.25 million investment in just 13 weeks. The London production moved to the Novello Theatre in 2012, where it still plays. It also inspired a UK reality show called Mamma Mia! I Have a Dream, which served as a competition to find the show's lead actors.

Ulvaeus was uncertain about the wild success of the Mamma Mia! musical: "You never know beforehand if something is going to be a hit or not. Before the release of Dancing Queen, I had no idea if it was going to be a hit!"

Martha Banta, current associate director of the US touring version of the musical Mamma Mia! and former associate director for Mamma Mia! on Broadway, feels the show's script is key to its success and longevity. "The story has kept the show going," she says. She explains that the show has a "multigenerational appeal," appealing to both mothers and daughters, for example. The audience is invited to find out the real dad of the daughter in the show, and that's not revealed until the show's end. The show has "identifiable characters." Unlike other musicals, the order of the show's music isn't revealed beforehand, surprising the audience and keeping the excitement high, especially if you're an ABBA fan. She adds that the "mega mix of three songs" at the show's end gives you an outlet to party your way out the door. The music tops off the show. Ultimately, she notes that "the musical Mamma Mia! hasn't been a star vehicle show." ABBA is the star of the show. Although the show has excellent theatre actors, they're not widely known by people. The current US touring production of the musical Mamma Mia! opened in Denver in October. Banta also feels the show's producer (Judy Craymer) and the entire production company have been really terrific to work with.

Banta has observed a higher level of interactivity with the current US touring production of Mamma Mia! "There's more singing along, clapping, interaction, and dancing this time."

She believes Mamma Mia! has played a key role in sustaining ABBA's career after they stopped touring and recording. In her experience, many younger people were introduced to ABBA through the musical Mamma Mia!

Phyllida Lloyd, director of the Mamma Mia! musical, underlines the centrality of ABBA's music to the musical: "The (ABBA) songs are part of our cultural heritage."

A third Mamma Mia! film has been discussed but hasn't been confirmed yet. Judy Craymer said in 2023, "She's sure the (third) film will happen. I'm in the privileged position that I have Universal Studios wanting to do it, who I love working with, and I have a storyline." Meryl Streep, Colin Firth, Amanda Seyfried, and Pierce Brosnan have committed in principle to appear in that film, should it move forward. But Björn Ulvaeus appears pessimistic that the film will ever materialize, at least in the same format: "People want to do it. Universal (Music Group) wants to do it. Judy Craymer wants to do it. But there's not going to be another Mamma Mia! film. That's just wishful thinking."

The Mamma Mia! musical helped spawn two film spinoffs—Mamma Mia! The Movie and the sequel Mamma Mia! Here We Go Again. Mamma Mia! The Movie, which boasted such stars as Meryl Streep, Pierce Brosnan, Christine Baranski, and Colin Firth, opened in London on June 30, 2008, and is reportedly "the most successful film musical ever," as well as "the highest-grossing movie of all time at the UK and Irish box offices." Streep was particularly enamored with playing the role of Donna. In addition to being a lifelong ABBA fan, she found that the Mamma Mia! musical had a healing and uplifting effect on her after the 9/11 tragedy in New York. Benny Andersson and Björn Ulvaeus even had small roles in the first film—Andersson appeared as the Dancing Queen piano player, and Ulvaeus was cast for just an instant as a Greek god. The film was largely shot on the Greek island of Skiathos, with Donna's villa shot on the 007 stage at Pinewood Studios. Mamma Mia! Here We Go Again was released in 2018 and helped drive up sales of ABBA's Gold —Greatest Hits album in the UK soon afterward. Sales of ABBA records also rose in the US around that time.

When Hollywood offered to buy the film rights to Mamma Mia!, Judy Craymer insisted on producing the picture herself. As she recounts, "There was no way I was going to sell the rights and have someone else do it." She fought the suggestions of other experienced directors, such as Steven Spielberg, to take over. She also insisted on bringing along Catherine Johnson as the writer and Phyllida Lloyd as the film's director.

A third Mamma Mia! film has been discussed but hasn't been confirmed yet. Judy Craymer said in 2023, "She's sure the (third) film will happen. I'm in the privileged position that I have

Universal Studios wanting to do it, who I love working with, and I have a storyline." Meryl Streep, Colin Firth, Amanda Seyfried, and Pierce Brosnan have committed in principle to appear in that film, should it move forward. But Björn Ulvaeus appears pessimistic that the film will ever materialize, at least in the same format: "People want to do it. Universal (Music Group) wants to do it. Judy Craymer wants to do it. But there's not going to be another Mamma Mia! film. That's just wishful thinking."

According to Magnus Palm, "Mamma Mia! is divorced from ABBA themselves because the songs have been put in a new context and mean something else when they're in Mamma Mia! performed by these other singers. But it's one of many things that's constantly going on to keep ABBA's music and the ABBA phenomenon in the spotlight."

Chapter 5

Expanding the ABBA Brand- Multimedia and Interactive Extensions of ABBA

Given the inherent interactive element in ABBA's shows and the insatiable appetite of ABBA fans for more ABBA music, band background information, and paraphernalia, it's unsurprising that carefully controlled multimedia extensions of their music have helped accelerate their continuing popularity. These extensions add new dimensions to the band, including cultural and historical contexts, and establish an even stronger bond between the band and its fans. The band lives on in multimedia environments and experiences, even when they're not physically present. These multimedia experiences play a key role in cross-promoting ABBA's music and further propelling ABBA's mania.

As Carl Magnus Palm mentions, one of the most amazing aspects of the band's revival success from the 1990s onward is that they enjoyed great popularity without touring, unlike most other bands. They found different ways to funnel their music—through the Mamma Mia! musicals, the ABBA Voyage show, and the interactive Mamma Mia! restaurant parties, which all succeeded, he points out. One of the band's advantages in this regard is that their music was already in party mode and conveys a feeling of happiness and letting loose, he stresses. As a result, they were able to exploit these new properties in a way that wouldn't be possible with bands like the Beatles, he maintains. Based on these efforts, "ABBA essentially extended their brand, made the brand stronger, and kept the music alive," Palm believes.

"Another factor that probably influenced the band to expand into other ventures relating to their music is that a number of ABBA tribute bands appeared on the scene and profited from the ABBA brand, but ABBA itself didn't benefit from shows of those bands other than receiving royalties," according to him.

One of the most prominent multimedia extensions of ABBA's music is the ABBA Voyage show, which serves as an extension to ABBA's Voyage album. Some of the album's material is actually old, but spruced up. One of those songs is "Just a Notion." According to Ulvaeus, "Wikipedia says the song was recorded in September 1978, which sounds about right. That puts it between ABBA the Album and Voulez-Vous, and it would have been included in the latter had we not decided against it. Why did we decide against it? In hindsight, I don't have a clue. It's a good song with great vocals. I know that we played it to a publisher in France and a couple of other people we trusted, and they liked it very much as far as I can remember. So it's a mystery and will remain a mystery. Benny has recorded a new backing track to which we've added drums and guitars, but all the vocals are from the original 1978 tracks. In a way, it demonstrates what we plan to do with ABBA Voyage in 2022. We will have a live band playing there, but all the vocals will be from the old recordings."

In the ABBA Voyage show, ABBA performs 18-22 hits as ABBA -tars (virtual avatars) without the need to be physically present, essentially enabling them, through pre-recordings, to play the songs accompanied by a live band and backing singers performing at a specially designed London arena for the show. According to Ludvig Andersson, one of the show's co-producers, the songs are assembled as a "setlist for a concert, not a 'Best-of' karaoke session—they're not just the 'ABBA Gold' hits." As such, there will be opportunities for the setlist to change.

Two songs from the Voyage album were included in the show— "Don't Shut Me Down" and [missing song].

Andersson initially expressed a preference for including the new songs in the show: "I talked to Bjorn. I said, if we would have been doing this for real, going out on the stage, we would have added a couple of new songs to perform. And then I called the ladies, and they said yes. That surprised me a lot. I think they saw the whole picture, and it would be good for the ABBA Voyage concert if we had some new music out there. So we did that, and I thought with the first two songs, it went so well, and they could still sing, and we could still produce music in the studio, so we said maybe we'll do a couple of others while we're at it, and we ended up doing a whole album."

The show utilizes 3D holographic images that "de-age" the band, telescoping them back to the 70s. The band virtually dons' costumes created by Dolce & GABBA— that are in the spirit of their 70s costumes but not facsimiles of them. As Bjorn Ulvaeus jocularly notes, "the white dungarees are not there." Anni-Fried Lyngstad assures fans that "there are some over-the-top costumes in the show, too. Why not? It would have been odd to transform our flamboyant side into something safe. That wouldn't be us, would it?"

Ulvaeus had an interesting perspective on transforming into and viewing his virtual ABBA -tar: "I feel it's HIM from the 70s because I've been exposed to him almost daily for the past 40 years. It was easier to do if I looked at myself as a kind of historical figure, as 'him.' Even though it's me, it's him at the same time."

At the same time, the band initially had some trepidation about venturing into uncharted and unfamiliar territory with the ABBA Voyage show. As Ulvaeus acknowledged at the beginning of the process, "It's an immense risk, and most people I talk to don't appreciate that. Sometimes, I wake up at four in the morning and think, 'What the hell have we done?' I was nervous up until the first preview with an audience, but then, when I saw it with an audience, I knew it was working. It's amazing—it has surpassed any dream I could ever have had. We've somehow reached new generations by some miracle. I don't know how, but there you are. The film Mamma Mia! I suppose it played a role in that. There are new generations coming along. It feels good to be at the forefront of technology, but technology is just one part of it. There are so many other moving parts. Sometimes, there's talent; there are good songs. There's all of that behind it—but there's also luck. You have to be lucky when something works as well as this, as well as having the resources artistically, financially, and so forth."

Ulvaeus explains his enduring songwriting partnership with Andersson in light of the Voyage album and ABBA Voyage show: "First of all, both of us are still willing to take risks, to take another step forward, like we're doing with Voyage. Not so much the album, but the actual show in London. We've always tried to go into uncharted waters—like when we split up with ABBA and tried our hands at musicals. We still have something to give each other. Very often, in songwriting teams, one of the teams stagnates and writes the same thing over and over again, and then they don't work. But we work because we're still enjoying it. I don't know anyone better to work with, and hopefully, he feels the same. Of course, we have the fantastic advantage of having the same frames of reference. I just need to say a word, and he knows exactly what I'm thinking— what song I'm thinking about, what genre, and so forth."

Ulvaeus elaborates further on the writing process on Voyage: "We decided early on that if we recorded new songs, we would write the best songs we could, not by glancing at what other people are doing right now, but just by tapping into our own resources. The songs are timeless in that sense—we could have written them long ago."

The band perceived a special advantage in virtually performing in the ABBA Voyage show without the need to perform live, as Benny Andersson underlined: "We got sort of turned on by the thought that we could actually be onstage without us being there. The show is the first of its kind, which is why we were turned on by it. We thought, 'Wow, can we really do this?' It was good that we had some stamina because there had been some uphill battles during these five and a half years. We said, 'Well, we've started it. We need to go through with it, and it has to happen.' Everything, from ILM's work to the lighting to the sound, is amazingly beautiful. It's the best sound you've heard in an arena ever; I promise you that. That has been my department. I mean, the music is my department, the band's sound. All the people who work with this have been wonderful. But the technique has nothing to do with the show. You sit there and see a band, and that's what it is."

Andersson notes the selection of some lesser-known songs in the ABBA Voyage set: "We realized we could not play the hits, but we also wanted to give the concert some dynamics, so there are a few songs the audience will not be too familiar with, but we like them, so we put them in. It's 21 songs, and it feels good."

Agnetha Fältskog underscored the uncertainty about the experience of working on the Voyage show but also the joy of working on it: "None of us probably know what to expect, but we've worked with it a lot, so you grow into it eventually. We stand there doing these songs with, I don't know how many cameras and people. It felt great to do because it was so different. And there was a vibe—one felt maybe it's the last thing we do. Same thing with the album."

Ulvaeus believes "copies of ourselves, avatars, will go on living after we're dead, and that's the way of the future." He adds, "Lots of artists are going to be studying us, definitely."

Baillie Walsh, the show's director, stresses that he wanted to underplay the technology element and emphasize the emotional aspect: "The whole thing I fought against is the tech. I didn't want this to be a technological wonderland. The tech should be the least important thing, and it should not be visible. I wanted this to be an emotional experience and a concert. I wanted people to laugh, dance, and cry. And you've got to be really careful with that. It's multi-layered because you are playing with the past, present, and the future. And all those big questions. You can't throw that in people's faces. The concert isn't a big intellectual idea. But I knew there were a lot of big ideas under the surface. There's a lightness of touch to it that's very appealing."

Walsh advocated for the show to be "a live event with life-size avatars" rather than a cinematic project, which was the original idea. He wanted to "make the show as much of a gig as we possibly can."

The show has been a resounding success, "generating over $2 million a week and selling over 2,000,000 tickets. It has been a major attraction for overseas guests, who account for 25% of the attendees," according to Svana Gisla, co-producer of the ABBA Voyage show. In addition, "80% of those overseas attendees come to London just to see the show," she reports.

Ludvig Andersson, son of Benny Andersson and producer of the ABBA Voyage show, explains the show's aim: "The original concept of the show came from a very simple question—if we're going to do something with ABBA, but ABBA isn't physically there, what should we do? ABBA Voyage is what came of that. I've spent years trying to explain to people that it's not about trying to trick people into thinking ABBA is really there. It has nothing to do with that. It's about simply creating a piece of art that you step into. It's an experience on an emotional level. And that was all that mattered to us, to create something that could be felt."

Andersson elaborates further about the show's focus: "Yes, it's just a concert. But it took a really long time to make, and a lot of love and effort went into making it. A lot of people say they are struck by thoughts of aging, youth, time passing, and even death—not in a negative way, but in a beautiful and uplifting way. The show is all based on emotion. How does it feel? And how will the audience feel? That was always our number one priority—our most important guiding light."

Andersson adds: "I don't know exactly why ABBA Voyage has been so successful. On a simple level, I'd say it's been successful because it's very good. But it takes a lot of luck and a lot of work. I'd say the show is more than the sum of its parts. The first element is obviously the music. Then there are the visual elements, which present images of qualities like aging, time passing, and youth. There's a subliminal message. I think we did well. It's been a labor of love. The show allows people to share their emotions in a community-like environment, like a church. The show is a mirror of your expectations.

It wasn't done to make money, and it wasn't created by some corporation. It was created by ABBA itself and the team around them. As a result, we've had the freedom to do what we wanted, and I think we created something beautiful."

Svana Gisla notes, "We made the choice not to go digital with this show. We had lots and lots of people telling us we were mad to be spending all this money and creating the show for people to have to travel to a location, 3,000 at a time, to experience it. They didn't understand why we weren't showing millions of people around the world. But the answer to that, for us, was very simple—we wanted an emotional experience." For that reason, photography and filming are banned at the show in order to ensure the audience is present and they can experience things without putting phones in front of their eyes.

Gisla observes, "Everything about this show was unusual, and therefore, the creative process was unusual. There were several different work streams. Creating ABBA digitally took a long time, with over 1,000 VFX artists. We had to build the arena, which is a whole process in itself, including finding land, planning permissions, and architects. It was an enormous beast, to be honest, with a massive orchestra to conduct. We had fantastic people in every corner and still do. They all contributed enormously. It was a joint effort in the greatest sense of that phrase. It really was humongous, but it was a very joyful and happy process. We didn't really have a bad day; it was just so much fun. I think remnants of that live in the show, as it was created with a lot of joy and love by many very talented people." She claims the show "was always a creative venture, never a business venture."

"We looked at absolutely everything and did a lot of testing until we chose all the tech pieces. It was great to collaborate with lighting artists from all over Europe. We didn't leave any stones unturned in finding the best possible procurement and people."

Gisla provided details on the motion capture shoots for the show: "We did two very big motion capture shoots—one in Sweden and the other in London. The one in Sweden was done right before the first COVID lockdown. The second one was very complicated. We did the first film shoot in

London after the lockdown in September 2020, with 50 people on set. It required a lot of planning, but we got through it, which was a miracle in and of itself."

She recounts her initial meeting with Industrial Light & Magic about the ABBA Voyage project: "I just walked into their office with a storyboard in the beginning and was welcomed by Ben Morris, their creative director, and Sue Lyster, their executive in charge. They welcomed us and said, 'We've been waiting for something like this; our technology is capable of this now. It's obviously pushing every single boundary, and we're going to invent some stuff, but the technology is there, and we think we can do a great job with this.' Then we had the resources of some of the world's most talented visual effects artists. We ended up using three or four of their studios internationally."

Gisla notes, "The tech itself isn't new, but the way in which we've used it, the scale, and the barriers we've broken are new. I'm sure others will follow and are planning to follow."

Ludvig Andersson adds, "I think when ILM was presented with this idea, they were keen because they realized it was something they had never done before, and it was something basically that no one had done before. The project took up ten times as much processing power as the Star Wars movies. So it was also the biggest thing they had ever done."

As Andersson underscored, a central part of the project involved building a specific arena: "We realized we needed to construct our own venue to house ABBA Voyage. We can't fit this anywhere else; we can't tour it around. The physical building came from the metaphysical idea of what the show would be. We started on the stage and built outwards, and that became the arena."

ABBA Voyage used five different lighting systems to align and match physical and digital light. As Gisla points out, "Our lighting rig in the roof had to be redesigned three times to a point where it became so big it's actually very difficult to move. We will move eventually, I'm sure, but it's not a flat pack."

Gisla underscores ABBA's key role in the show's success: "It starts right there. It starts not just with their music but with them as people. They're very creative, generous, and brilliant, obviously. They were involved in every step of the process. There's not a single costume piece that ABBA didn't approve. Baillie Walsh (the show's director) sent them all of his lighting ideas for their approval. It's got their spirit, sensibilities, and them ingrained in it. They chose to be on that stage, and more than that, they put themselves there and put the work in to be there. It's very genuinely them."

Reportedly, the show "has sold over 2,000,000 tickets." It has been a major attraction for overseas guests, who account for "25% of the attendees." In addition, "80% of those overseas attendees come to London just to see the ABBA Voyage show."

Baillie Walsh also lauded ABBA for their role in the show's creation: "I think ABBA was the best band to do this with. First of all, because they were involved. And, without an artist's involvement, it possibly becomes a cynical money-making exercise. ABBA's motive for doing this was creative. They're creatively curious."

Stany Van Wymeersch believes the Voyage album and ABBA Voyage show "have been very important in continuing the incredible ABBA story. They represent the final contribution to that story and have brought the ABBA story to a conclusion in the most fantastic way. They're reaching new audiences with the Voyage show, even reaching audiences that never saw the Mamma Mia! musical. The show allows the band to present themselves in a contemporary way and is a totally new experience. ABBA reached new heights with this show. They're a cool band now." Many musical stars have seen the Voyage show, "including Brian May, Rod Stewart, Bruce Springsteen, and the Foo Fighters." Van Wymeersch emphasizes that, due to the ABBA show, "people can't underestimate ABBA anymore."

Plans are afoot to bring ABBA Voyage to North America, Australia, and Asia. As Gisla reports, "We're talking to quite a lot of potential partners in exactly those locations. We're not quite there, but we're looking at different options. I'm hoping that in a few months, we'll be in a position to pinpoint those locations. We would love to open more arenas. In Australia, specifically, there's a lot of love for ABBA and vice versa, and the same is true for North America. We are looking at Vegas, New York, and all the obvious places. Maybe even another one in Europe one day. There's a lot of appetite for the show coming from lots of different places."

In her view, Las Vegas would be a particularly suitable location for the ABBA Voyage show. As she explains, "We have live musicians, so we keep our band and do seven shows over five days a week. But you could roll around the clock. Vegas will quickly adopt this style of entertainment, and so will Elvis or the Beatles."

Ludvig Andersson adds: "We don't have firm plans yet to produce ABBA Voyage in other locations, but we've talked to many potential partners in such countries as the US, Australia, and Japan. It's complex to assemble a project like this. For one thing, we'd need to build our own arenas in these other locations."

Ulvaeus sums up his feelings about the show this way: "I've seen the show so many times, and I think we look good up there. But I have no idea what it really is that makes people have it in them to want to listen to music that was done 50 years ago, 40 years ago, 30 years ago. Back in '79, I don't think we ever thought about being listened to in 10 years' time. If you said something like this would happen in 50 years' time, it would be preposterous. It just doesn't happen."

Another special aspect of the show was ABBA's partnership with Wallenius, a Swedish shipping company behind the Ocean bird wind-powered vessels. Andersson called attention to the value of this partnership: "I believe we must be at the forefront of what music and entertainment can be with ABBA Voyage, and it is extremely pleasing to be able to make it happen in partnership with Ocean bird and Wallenius, who are as keen on sustainability as we are."

One hundred sixty cameras were used in the show to scan the bodies of ABBA, recording their every movement and facial expression, which the designers then used as the basis for the avatars driving the live show. Body doubles were used in the motion capture process to give the digital band—represented in their late 1970s prime- with glitzy sequined costumes and winged catsuit outfits designed by B. Åkerlund and Dolce & GABBA—a more youthful presence. Over 1,000 visual effects artists and one billion computing hours went into making the ABBA -tars as realistic and human-like as possible. During the show, they appear on huge 65-million-pixel screens, often as life-sized versions of their younger selves. At other times, the four musicians are shown in photorealistic close-ups on the larger screens that loom over the dance floor and surrounding seats.

Kevin Williams, founder of the out-of-home entertainment consultancy KWP, believes "this show breaks many of the boundaries for live audience engagement. The fact that Industrial Light and Magic were able to elicit such a compelling and positive reaction from the performers for the holographic stage performance shows how far the technology has advanced. The audience's reaction to the sold-out shows proves this is a strong and compelling experience, though the limitations of the technology used still show that continued investment in this application will be needed. Not only does this show bring new performances to the stage, but it also offers new kinds of experiences.

The ability to attract a cross-generational audience with this immersive performance, including appealing to new and old audiences, is a great way to reinvigorate the ABBA brand. Considering some of the band's physical limitations at this point, this immersive performance reinvigorates the brand beyond all other experiences, as demonstrated by increased album and merch sales. However, the event's cost must be weighed against the show's accomplishments. We have yet to see the event roll out to other localities, at which point we'll get a better idea of the show's impact on the ABBA brand beyond the UK."

ABBA is a true supergroup, like the Beatles, and the ABBA Voyage show has had a major impact on the music and the audience that supports it. The fact that the technology used in the show was applied with the group's support is a great testament to the opportunities that virtual and immersive performances hold in "time-traveling" popular performers. This is best illustrated by the immersive Elvis experience in development by Layered Reality and rumors of other performers looking at the ABBA experience as a blueprint for future performances.

Sarah Wiggins puts the ABBA Voyage show in a larger context. She says, "ABBA illustrates perfectly how changing times can present opportunity. Rather than simply trying to repeat their heyday, they're blending who they were then with how they are now. Their tunes are just as catchy, but the sentiments of their lyrics have shifted to reflect a new set of emotions and life experiences."

Additional promotion of ABBA's music connected with the release of the Voyage album and show was provided temporarily on ABBA Radio in 2021, which ran from November 5 to November 14 that year on satellite channel 54 and from November 5 to December 4 that year via the SiriusXM app. ABBA songs from their earliest period up to 2021 were played on those channels, along with solo material from band members and cover versions of ABBA's best-known hits. In addition, Andersson and Ulvaeus provided commentary on the Voyage album, the ABBA Voyage show, and the band's earlier material and music before ABBA.

ABBA The Museum in Stockholm, which opened in 2013, has provided an important overview of the band's background and evolution through interactive exhibits and experiences. The museum was partly an outgrowth of the ABBA World Exhibition that toured Europe and Australia from 2009 to 2011, stopping in cities such as London.

There was another key impetus behind the museum's establishment. Mattias Hansson, former managing director of the museum, felt that "from a Swedish state point of view, it should have been around for many years because it's one of the most famous Swedish brands ever. We knew from the tourism office in Stockholm that each and every year, they receive thousands of questions from tourists about where to go to see something about ABBA. For years, they have been forced to say 'nowhere.'" Ulvaeus played a key role in the museum's creation, prompting Hansson to say, "For certain, Bjorn Ulvaeus is the brightest creative mind I've ever been in the room with."

At the museum's entrance, visitors are treated to ABBA music videos, providing new opportunities to interact with and perform with the band's music. The museum includes the group's stage costumes and several audio and video stations where visitors can perform the band's music. It even allows visitors to play the role of a fifth member of the group. Located near the Gröna Lund theme park on the island of Djurgården in Stockholm, the museum occupies three levels.

The band members recount their experiences via audio guides prepared by Johnson, creator of the Mamma Mia! musicals.

A section called "5th Member" allows visitors to perform one of ABBA's hit songs as a fifth member alongside life-sized holographic images of the band. These songs include "Waterloo," "Dancing Queen," "Mamma Mia," "Money, Money, Money," and "The Winner Takes It All."

Visitors can also try on ABBA costumes virtually using a motion-sensing device.

In another section called "ABBA Quiz," visitors are quizzed on their knowledge of ABBA trivia. Additionally, ABBA karaoke allows visitors to sing their favorite ABBA songs as part of an audition in what seems like a recreated Polar Studio.

The museum incorporates fun and novelty elements relating to their songs. For example, one exhibit called "Ring Ring" features a phone connected to an outside line that occasionally rings with a member of the group on the other end. Only the band members know the number.

There are also more personalized exhibits that foster stronger connections between the band and its audience/fans.

To immerse visitors more deeply in the ABBA experience, the museum features exhibits such as the Hep Stars tour camper van and the helicopter shown on the cover of the Arrival album.

Visitors also have the opportunity to hear interviews with the ABBA members, their clothing designer, and their manager.

The museum presents the early family and musical backgrounds of each band member, including photos of family members and recollections of their solo performances early on.

One of the most intriguing aspects of the museum is its success in unearthing insights about the band's musical motivations and drive for success. Visitors learn that Ulvaeus attributed his ambition to do well in part to "the effects of witnessing my father's need to work for his brother after his business went bankrupt." One exhibit also highlights how Anni-Frid's path to music at a young age was partly paved by support from her grandmother after her mother passed away at a very young age. She recounts "how she got all the lead vocals in my school choir most of the time, and I joined my first dance band when I was only 13 years old. That changed my life."

The museum provides a revealing behind-the-scenes look at the band's rise to success, beginning with their performance of "Waterloo" at the 1974 Eurovision Song Contest. In the "Titled Songs" section, the signature piano and horn sounds of the celebrated hit lead visitors into the exhibit. It includes images of the band's performance at the event, a stage displaying the costumes they wore, and the gold guitar played by Ulvaeus. A diary from Benny Andersson during Eurovision, originally published in the Swedish newspaper Expressen, is also reproduced on the wall. The section highlights the challenges the band faced before their performance, including sound problems during rehearsals and Andersson's heightened anxiety just before going on stage. The band's Eurovision gold medal and the original printing of the 1974 "Waterloo" single are displayed at the center of the room.

Another exhibit, Folkparken, features the space where the band first performed and met.

The Creating the Songs exhibit provides a window into the different approaches to songwriting taken by Andersson and Ulvaeus. It includes recreations of the beach house on the Swedish island of Viggso, where Ulvaeus and Andersson wrote "Dancing Queen" and "Fernando."

Another section offers glimpses into Polar Studio in Stockholm, where many of ABBA's biggest hits were recorded.

Full details of the band's touring process and stage preparations are displayed in "The Performing on Stage" exhibit, including their tour itineraries with maps, concert memorabilia such as costumes, programs, and security badges. A 1979 stage rider is also displayed in this section, specifying the band's requirements for a 7-foot Steinway grand piano, two dressing rooms with large mirrors, and beverages such as Coca-Cola, tea, coffee, and milk.

The museum devotes the last exhibit, Slipping Through My Fingers, to the issues leading to the band's dissolution. Ulvaeus frankly acknowledges his changing perspective regarding the rearing of his children with Faltskog towards the end of the ABBA tours: "Agnetha hated leaving the children for even a very short period of time. I guess I was irritated back then and didn't quite understand her. It was just a few days, for heaven's sake. But I do understand her now. We both loved them just as much, but I was constantly on the run into a potentially glorious future while she was in the here and now with our children." Andersson also acknowledges the possible damage to the two couples in the band due to their constant work together in ABBA: "I know I've said before that ABBA was keeping the couples together, but possibly it could be true the other way around."

The museum includes a gift shop with items such as mugs, posters, vinyl records, and "Dancing Queen" T-shirts, as well as a section devoted to the band members' projects outside ABBA.

The museum also includes a theater, which typically shows movies from ABBA concerts and other ABBA-related content. In addition, special events and tours on various ABBA topics, including a talk on ABBA costumes, have been organized at the museum.

The museum provides more cultural and historical context for the group's music. It features key milestones, sites, and instruments relating to the development and history of ABBA's music, including:

- An exhibit called "Waterloo," depicting Brighton at the time of the 1974 Eurovision Song Contest, including items from the seminal event.

- An exhibit recreating The Polar Studio, where ABBA recorded much of their later music. Many items used in the studio are prominently displayed.

- Benny's piano—a self-playing piano linked to Benny's own piano in his home, that essentially plays when he does.

- Folkpark—a recreation of the place where ABBA originally met.

- Audio guides—an audio-guided tour written by Catherine Johnson, the writer of the screenplay for the Mamma Mia! film.

- Ring Ring—a special phone that only the four members of ABBA know the number to.

In essence, these experiences afford visitors deeper immersion in ABBA's cultural artifacts and the creation of ABBA's music.

Other temporary exhibitions borrowing elements from ABBA The museum has been launched since its founding.

Stany Van Wymeersch was a consultant on the official ABBA Super Troupers exhibition at the O2 Arena in London that ran from December 2019 to March 2020, providing panel texts, quotes, and background information for the exhibition. Jude Kelly was the exhibition's curator, working closely with Bjorn and ABBA The Museum. Each room in the exhibition centered around one ABBA album, and the exhibition provided a social and economic context for ABBA's music.

In addition, the museum has integrated and extended its experience into Spotify.

A 60-minute walking tour called The ABBA The Museum Walk around Djurgarden Island complements a visit to the museum. Visitors have a chance on the tour to take in key sites relevant to ABBA 's career and stop at key locations where ABBA was photographed. The tour concludes at the ABBA museum

Social media has played a key role in introducing ABBA to younger generations. The key role of TikTok in promoting ABBA's music and reaching younger fans is underlined by the fact that "according to the Ice 36 blog, over 520,000 TikTok videos incorporate ABBA music in some fashion. 'Dancing Queen,' in particular, has become a part of TikTok trends. In response to their overwhelming TikTok popularity, ABBA themselves contributed to TikTok in 2021 and released a special piano version of 'Dancing Queen' on the platform, according to Billboard."

Paul Hourican, TikTok's former head of music operations, addressed this phenomenon: "With one of the most recognizable music catalogs ever created, ABBA's unique craft of songwriting truly transcends generations and has inspired music lovers for decades. Our community has already shown us with their own creations that this is the music they've been waiting for, and we're excited to see how ABBA can inspire a new generation of fans, sparking yet another wave of creativity with the hits that have defined pop for so long."

Now, ABBA has even entered the pinball world, with the release of a pinball game called ABBA Pinball by Pinball Brothers in May 2024, which comes in two editions—the Voyage Collector edition and the Arrival Limited edition. The Voyage game uses assets from the Voyage holographic stage show running in London. It challenges players to power up the ABBA tars so that they can open up the portal to the Voyage dimension, where the ancient Medallion of Power is the magic key during the journey. To create the ABBA tars, players must gather the band members' instruments, outfits, and souls. Players have a chance to time travel to the 70s and 80s and follow ABBA's footsteps during their tours in Sweden, the Nordics, Europe, the USA, Australia, and Japan. They can then enter the Voyage dimension, where they can search for the Medallion of Power, conquer three multiball battles, and face the final wizard mode. The game features more than 20 of ABBA's top songs, paired with exclusive visuals from the ABBA Voyage show in London. The game features a disco mirror ball and an interactive "Arrival helicopter" from the iconic album cover. The ABBA pinball game represents an interesting new extension of the brand, as the band's music and career seem well-suited to the pinball game form.

Interestingly, Ludvig Andersson, a pinball fan himself, originally brought the idea of an ABBA-themed pinball machine to David Janson, CEO of Pinball Brothers. He provides background on the game's germination: "I was an avid pinball fan growing up and realized there should be an ABBA pinball game. ABBA and pinball go well together. The ABBA pinball game was fun to do and something we could do on the side. One of the other reasons for entering the pinball market is that pinball games were popular in the 70s."

The production and development of the ABBA pinball game has taken longer than the ABBA Voyage show—it's taken almost 7 years to finally come to fruition. Actually, I haven't seen the finished product yet. The pinball project kept changing over the years. It first started when I attended a conference and asked the audience who they'd recommend as a developer of a pinball game for ABBA, and someone mentioned Daniel Janson, CEO of Pinball Brothers. So, I called him, and we got started on the project. There are two versions of the game—one called Voyage and the other called Arrival. I think pinball games are an art form that combines graphic design, digital design, and game design.

Pinball Brothers highlighted the game's tribute to ABBA's legacy: "This ABBA Adventure is our way of congratulating our national musical treasure on turning 50, and our way of saying 'Thank you for the music.'"

In another key example of cross-promotion for the ABBA brand, a temporary exhibition called the ABBA Voyage Exhibition opened in May 2023 and will run until at least 2025. The exhibition shows the making of ABBA's Voyage album and the groundbreaking virtual concert experience. The exhibit also features exclusive interviews and footage, as well as stage costumes by B. Akerlund in collaboration with designers such as Dolce & Gabba and Michael Schmidt.

A temporary "ABBA World" exhibition ran in Malmö from April 29 to May 12, 2024. The exhibition included sections, elements, and experiences from ABBA The Museum, the ABBA Voyage show, the Mamma Mia! films, Mamma Mia! The Party, and Polar Music International.

In addition, the Foundation ABBA The Museum was established "to preserve and publicly display, and through other means, make objects of all kinds available relating to ABBA and to Swedish music life. The foundation receives and administers donations of objects relevant to its purpose. The foundation accepts monetary contributions in order to purchase objects available for sale on the market when an opportunity arises. In the future, the foundation will contribute to making submitted theses, scanned newspaper clippings, etc., publicly available as working materials for students, scientists, or the media (via login)."

The Backstage Hotel (formerly Pophouse Hotel) in Stockholm offers a convenient travel point for ABBA fans and further immersion into the ABBA experience. The hotel, which is integrated into the ABBA Museum complex, includes an ABBA-themed room called the ABBA Gold Suite, named after the ABBA Gold album. The walls of the ABBA Gold Suite are decorated with gold records and CDs from the band. According to Sandra Miller Klinge, Director of Program and

Marketing for Cirkus Venues, "the ABBA Gold Suite room (at the Backstage Hotel) is highly appreciated by our guests."

Mamma Mia! The Party, an interactive party based on the play Mamma Mia!, offers another vibrant platform for exploiting the interactive nature of ABBA's music. The show, set in the Nikos-family Taverna on the island of Skopelos from the first Mamma Mia! film, affords participants a four-course meal and an opportunity to sing and dance in an ABBA disco afterward.

Ulvaeus explains the motivation for developing the interactive show: "I've been sitting in theaters around the globe since we started, and have experienced the happy mood in the audience, where people stand up in the aisles and dance and sing… This is the next extension from that—transfer the mood to a restaurant, a Greek restaurant, of course—have a gigantic party, and tell a story in real-time."

He adds: "This is an experiment, just like the musical was. This time around, the audience guests are part of a story in real-time, with not only song and dance being the ingredients but also food, wine, and environment. If it turns out the way I hope, there are no limits. It could become a very big party, indeed. We start at Djurgården in Stockholm, just a few years from where ABBA The Museum is located. A perfect fit for it."

It was initially introduced at Restaurant Tyrol in the Gröna Lund amusement park in Stockholm in January 2016 and subsequently ran in London and Amsterdam. It was later introduced at the O2 in London in 2020 after running for four years in Stockholm. The show is returning this August to Gröna Lund Park for a run until October 3. The play is set across two floors, complete with a fully mobile cast and live band. The performers deliver both the food and storyline, encouraging guests to join the drama as dancing queens themselves. Mamma Mia! The Party is produced by Björn Ulvaeus and Ingrid Sutej. The story was written by Calle Norlén, Roine Soderlundh, and Ulvaeus.

According to Norlén, "It's a separate story entirely of its own—about a fictional restaurant on the Greek island where the Mamma Mia! film was shot. To capitalize on the interest in the blockbuster movie, the restaurant owners decide to turn their taverna into a Mamma Mia!-themed party restaurant. There is no stage, and the action takes place in real-time among the guests.

The plot is basically that the owner couple, a Greek man with his daughter and a Swedish woman with her son, met during the filming. Their children fall in love with each other, which is considered slightly inappropriate, even though they are not blood relatives. Just like the film, the story is essentially a way of presenting ABBA songs in an entertaining context.

Since everything takes place in the audience, you automatically participate as much as you want. People sing along, learn to dance the Zorba, answer quiz questions at the tables, and dance on the dance floor afterward. The party is an approximately four-hour, all-evening concept."

Jessica Klingberg, general manager of "Mamma Mia! The Party," reports that "over 1,000,000 guests have attended our Swedish and London shows combined." The show has been performed so far "in Stockholm, Gothenburg, and London, and will open in Rotterdam in September." She says that "our guests are ecstatic when they leave, having had an experience of a lifetime. Each night ends with our guests dancing on the dance floor and singing to the songs. They love that they feel part of the show, get to eat delicious Greek food, and still have time to talk and socialize with their friends, while experiencing a Greek taverna on Skopelos, and enjoying a lot of ABBA music." According to Klingberg, "we quite often have groups of people with mixed ages-sometimes, we have families spanning three generations. The show appeals to people of all ages. In Sweden, however, the majority of guests are 40+, while in London, they are a bit younger."

According to Gareth Owen, sound engineer for Mamma Mia! The Party, "The use of spatial immersive audio is absolutely critical to the implementation of Mamma Mia! The Party. The performers are placed right in the audience; wherever the cast moves, they have audience members all around them. This creates a real problem for the sound team.

One of the golden rules of live sound engineering is never to put a microphone in front of a speaker. The result is rarely anything other than squealing feedback. Sound engineers spend their whole careers trying to avoid this at all costs. In Mamma Mia! The Party, not only are the cast microphones ALWAYS in front of a speaker, but they are usually in front of lots of speakers running at very high volumes. It is, to put it mildly, a massive sonic headache.

Immersive audio is critical to enveloping the audience in the experience and making the production work. We try to make sure that wherever you sit in the taverna, the sound of the cast and the band appears to come from the direction it ought to.

Key to the audience's enjoyment is that the show is presented at a volume where they can sing along in a fun and uninhibited way. By the time the show gets going, most audience members will be up on their feet, whirling their white napkins around their heads and singing along at the top of their voices. A key part of this is the quality and volume of the delivered sound."

Chapter 6

ABBA's Role as A Major Cultural Swedish Export

Although ABBA was always an enormously successful pop/rock band, it became a major Swedish cultural export and brand over time. The band was singled out for its role as a Swedish cultural export when it was awarded the Swedish Government's Music Export Prize in March 2021, following the release of their Voyage album. The Swedish government stated, "This year marks 50 years and over 400 million records sold since ABBA was formed. What Agnetha, Bjorn, Benny, and Anni-Frid started in 1972 was the first big step in the story of the global success of Swedish music. Thank you for the music."

Referring to ABBA 's worldwide success with their Voyage album, the government noted, "It is not every day that the BBC reschedules a news broadcast to premiere a new pop song. But that is exactly what happened when ABBA released new songs for the first time in 40 years. Suddenly, some of history's greatest pop artists were back. ABBA 's album Voyage was not only one of the greatest, most surprising, and acclaimed comebacks in pop history, but it also broke new records. The LP reached number 1 in 18 countries, topped the album chart in the US, and was the best-selling album in Germany. They were most successful in the UK. Only the Beatles and six other artists have reached number 1 more than the 10 times that ABBA reached in autumn 2021. Voyage became the fastest-selling album of the 21st century in the UK. In just three days, the group's much-discussed and spectacular avatar-based show in London sold a million tickets."

Anna Hallberg, Sweden's Minister for Foreign Trade and Nordic Affairs, added, "ABBA has symbolized globally successful Swedish music, and they have played a huge part in establishing Sweden internationally. Being able to return to the stage after 40 years is an extraordinary and immense feat."

ABBA: The Museum has been a major cultural and tourist attraction for Stockholm. Before the museum's opening, then-Stockholm mayor Kristina Axén Olin said, "We are convinced that this is important for both Stockholm citizens and for marketing the city."

Interestingly, ABBA wasn't promoted at all in the beginning by the Swedish government and cultural establishment, according to Carl Magnus Palm. He observes, "The band was actually quite controversial in Sweden, and got bad press, partly because they were super popular and very commercial. Their music was criticized at the time by the media and the cultural establishment in Sweden for being superficial and avoiding social and political issues. Those people viewed their music as simple pop music and not serious. In addition, the band's music was regarded as a business largely because of Stig Anderson's business approach. Since he planned their marketing strategy meticulously, the band was regarded more as a business venture than a musical entity, though Anderson also contributed to some of the band's lyrics. On the other hand, the Swedish people had some pride in ABBA."

Ola Johansson also underlines the changing attitudes in Sweden toward ABBA. Initially, he notes, "ABBA was a lightning rod and a controversial band due to what they represented about the commercialization of music at a time when the prevailing ideology in Swedish politics and culture was quite leftist." Over time, as political and social winds shifted, attitudes toward ABBA changed, and ABBA's commercial style of music was better accepted. There was a greater awareness of what ABBA accomplished and what it meant to people. In fact, Johansson believes that around the 1990s, the Swedish cultural industries were increasingly viewed as more important economic development tools, and the branding of music was better accepted. Now, all facets of the Swedish government support pop music in the country and aim to make Swedish music a global force through programs such as Export Sweden.

Before ABBA, Johansson believes, "Swedish pop musicians suffered from an inferiority complex, and their music was largely derivative of larger trends in Anglo-American pop music." He feels ABBA was different in several ways. In his view, their music wasn't really rock or R&B. They were inspired by an earlier form of pop music in Sweden and Europe. Their music had a lighter touch, was more focused on vocal harmonies, and less on the beat. They had simple melodies. The piano also played a big role in their music, greatly affecting their songwriting. Essentially, ABBA merged the more European style of pop music with rock music.

Johansson believes ABBA served as a role model for other Swedish pop bands. According to him, "They helped build an infrastructure for Swedish pop music. ABBA showed that Swedish pop music could gain traction on an international level, and the band served as a trigger for Swedish pop music to be commercially successful and have some artistic value as well. In addition, some people in and around ABBA remained active in the Swedish music business even after the band disbanded, and the band, in effect, trained other Swedish pop musicians in the process of music making."

Jared Raab believes ABBA helped drive Swedish pop music forward by showing Swedish pop musicians following them that they could break through internationally. They set a benchmark for other Swedish pop musicians. In fact, he feels Swedish pop music from artists like Max Martin changed the face of North American pop music in the '90s, as they worked with such top artists in the US and the UK as Britney Spears and the Backstreet Boys.

Victoria Norback believes ABBA put Swedish pop music on the map and opened the door internationally for other Swedish pop music. However, there were already famous Swedish pop musicians at the time. Additionally, ABBA's music helped people get to know Sweden.

The increasing impact of ABBA's music on Swedish culture has become evident. According to Maria Lexhagen, professor of tourism studies at Mid-Sweden University and former director of ETOUR, a tourism institute at the university, ABBA has been ingrained in the DNA of Swedish culture. For example, people in Sweden play ABBA at their weddings. ABBA even played "Dancing Queen" at the pre-wedding ceremony of King Carl XVI Gustaf of Sweden and the future Queen Silvia of Sweden in 1976. Additionally, the musical education system in Sweden is supported, in part, by homegrown bands, including ABBA. Lexhagen notes, "ABBA is still on everyone's radar, and they're pushing the limits of what you can expect from a band that hasn't performed or released new albums for decades."

The Rise of ABBA Tourism

Researchers at ETOUR coined the term "ABBA tourism" to symbolize the impact of ABBA 's music on tourism to Sweden by both fans and non-fans. Maria Lexhagen views this kind of tourism as part of the global trend towards fan travel to particular destinations induced by their attachment to various pop culture figures in literature, film, music, and other popular cultural phenomena connected with those locales. She characterizes fan attachment to particular pop culture figures as a manifestation of a fandom community and travels as part of fan practice. Lexhagen notes that this trend "is demand-driven and has evolved in unexpected and interesting ways for tourism.

She observes that "ABBA tourism has occurred in various places and has varied across time." Pop culture tourism can provide an opportunity for fans to engage with and interact with a band for an extended time, enjoying a more personalized experience with the band rather than just observing them. Traveling to a place connected with a band helps reinforce fan interest in and appreciation for the band. For example, by visiting ABBA The Museum in Stockholm, fans are allowed to make a tangible connection with the band. Through pop culture tourism, fans can also walk in the footsteps of their favorite pop culture figures.

Lexhagen highlights the important role technology has played in supporting pop culture by allowing fans to live virtually with a band for a longer time. She believes that immersive experiences in museums, such as those at ABBA The Museum, offer new, personalized ways for fans to experience ABBA's music. The multimedia features and immersive experiences, including audio guides narrated by the band, enable direct communication with fans. Additionally, the ABBA Voyage show helped rejuvenate interest in the band and was a factor in persuading ABBA fans to visit the show in London. This kind of experience combines physical touch experiences with high-tech elements.

Lexhagen has found that generational travel is an important aspect of tourism experiences connected with pop culture. She notes that newer fans are attracted to bands because of newer experiences with those bands. For example, younger fans became aware of and interested in ABBA through the ABBA Voyage show.

Studies conducted by the ETOUR center in 2013 highlighted the strong impact ABBA's music had on travel to Sweden and other locations by ABBA fans. According to that research, almost 8 out of 10 ABBA fans said they wouldn't have traveled to the specific destination they visited on their last ABBA journey if it hadn't been for their interest in the band, reports Lexhagen. In one striking finding, "5 out of 10 ABBA fans surveyed said they visited Sweden specifically because of ABBA." Furthermore, "8 out of 10 said that ABBA was the main reason for their ABBA-related journey, and in the case of visitors to the ABBA Museum, this number was 9 out of 10.

Additionally, 75% of the visitors to the ABBA Museum also visited other attractions in Stockholm, such as other museums and ABBA-related experiences like places, concerts, and musicals."

Christine Lundberg, a former researcher at ETOUR, noted that "this showed that the 'ABBA tourists' can be seen as cultural tourists who willingly take part in other ABBA-related experiences during their visit." Interestingly, their visits to the ABBA museum spurred most of them to plan additional visits. "8 out of 10 visitors planned on returning to the ABBA museum, and the majority said they would do so within a couple of years." A total of 96% of this group had recommended or planned to recommend the ABBA museum to others, indicating high satisfaction with their trip. "Almost 9 out of 10 of all the ABBA fans in the international survey said they are likely to visit Stockholm in the near future."

Lexhagen contends that ABBA tourism and other pop culture tourism experiences aren't simply limited to visiting particular locales and attractions related to pop culture figures. These experiences have driven fans to create their own events and develop new opportunities to meet each other through these shared experiences.

Mattias Hanson, the former managing director of the ABBA museum, emphasized the importance of the survey's results for the museum in 2013. ABBA the museum takes great interest in ETOUR's research on ABBA tourism, which keeps growing around the world due to different Mamma Mia! musicals and, of course, the ABBA museum. It's great to see pop culture finally take its place as part of our important history.

Tracey Beck, the executive director of the American Swedish Historical Museum, feels "ABBA made Americans more aware of Swedish pop music." Their impact was particularly significant because they were the first Swedish pop group to sing in English and set a standard that many other Swedish musicians followed. They opened the door for other Swedish pop acts in the American market and brought a "cool factor" to being Swedish because of their popularity. Beck also believes ABBA helped pave the way for other forms of Swedish entertainment, such as video games.

In her view, "the Mamma Mia! films and other productions helped revive interest in ABBA and introduced a newer generation to ABBA 's music," though the generation that grew up with ABBA never lost interest.

Beck reports that "the museum has held four ABBA dance parties since 2019, with some attendees replicating ABBA's costumes. In 2021, the museum partnered with the Philly POPS orchestra, which was doing a 'POPS Rocks ABBA: Mamma Mia! and More...' concert. The Philly POPS sent a small group to play live on the museum's terrace." Beck also noted that "a lot more younger people in their 20s attended our ABBA party this year."

ABBA's success has been a key factor behind Sweden's role as a net exporter of music. Reportedly, the only nations that are net exporters of music are the US, the UK, and Sweden.

Chapter 7

Tracking the Solo Music Careers of Agnetha Faltskog and Anni Frid Lyngstad During and Post ABBA

Agnetha Fältskog has explored diverse musical styles throughout her solo career after ABBA. One of her most successful solo albums was Wrap Your Arms Around Me, released in 1983 and produced by renowned producer Mike Chapman. Fältskog's first English-language solo album included the single "The Heat is On," which topped the Swedish and Norwegian pop charts and reached number two in the Netherlands and Belgium. Other singles, including "Wrap Your Arms Around Me" and "Can't Shake Loose," also appeared on the album. A CD version of the album was released in 2005, featuring five bonus tracks. "Can't Shake Loose," written by Russ Ballard, was released as the lead single in North America and became one of only two solo singles by Fältskog to hit the Billboard Hot 100 chart in the U.S., peaking at number 29. Fältskog also contributed the song "Man" to the album.

In 1987, Fältskog recorded the album I Stand Alone in Los Angeles, produced by Peter Cetera, former singer and bassist of the band Chicago. The album marked a departure from her previous two albums, adopting a "West Coast American" style. Cetera also performed a duet with Fältskog on the song "I Wasn't the One (Who Said Goodbye)." The track "Love in a World Gone Mad" was a cover of a song by British pop group Bucks Fizz.

Fältskog later recorded the album A, which included the first original material she had released since I Stand Alone. The album also featured her first self-penned track in almost 30 years, "I Keep Them on the Floor Beside My Bed."

A+, a reissued version of A, was released in October 2023 and consisted of 11 reimagined versions of the album's tracks, along with the single "Where Do We Go From Here," written by Fältskog. The A+ versions of "I Should Have Followed You Home," "Dance Your Pain Away," and "Perfume" were also included. Ten tracks were recorded for the album at Atlantis Studio in Stockholm, all written and recorded by Jörgen Elofsson. "When You Really Loved Someone" was released worldwide as a single from the album.

The album A features a wide variety of songs, including "I Should've Followed You Home," a duet with Gary Barlow, the piano ballad "I Was a Flower," and the disco-inspired track "Dance Your Pain Away."

Agnetha Fältskog shared her thoughts on revisiting the album, saying, "A couple of years ago, I heard one of the songs from my last album, A, on the radio. I have lots of fond memories from making that album, so I couldn't help but smile—time flies. Suddenly, it hit me: what would the album sound like if we made it today? I couldn't stop thinking about it. I reached out to the boys who produced A back in 2013: 'What would you guys think of reimagining A and making a totally new version of it?' They loved the idea. 'Let's try.' A while later, I heard the first reworked song, and I must say I absolutely loved it. It sounded so fresh and modern, even better than I imagined it!"

Regarding the recording of the song "Where Do We Go From Here?" for A+, Fältskog admitted she had concerns at first. The track was originally written by Swedish artist Kamila Bayrak. "Elofsson played the demo for me, and the demo was very good. Originally, it was another girl singing, and I said, 'I don't know if I can do this.' I was a bit tense and a bit nervous because, as you get older, your voice changes. I think my voice has dropped a little in tone or pitch, so I maybe sound a little more—well, not dark, but lower. But I still can express myself a lot, and I like to interpret the songs. And I did it, and I think it came out very well."

Fältskog's self-penned song, "I Keep Them on the Floor Beside My Bed," was a result of Elofsson's encouragement. She emphasized, "Jörgen kept saying, 'You have to write a song for this record.' I hadn't written any music in a long, long time. But I sat at the piano, and suddenly, it was there. A friend of mine said a lovely thing: 'It's in your spine. Even if you feel tired, when it's time, it will be there.'"

An animated music video was released alongside "Where Do We Go From Here," showcasing elements from Fältskog's life, including a replica of the Triumph Spitfire car she owned in the 1960s, which she used to drive between her home in Jönköping and Stockholm while ABBA was recording. The video, created by Aarto Hiiemaa, also features Fältskog's dogs and pays homage to iconic ABBA outfits, including a blue star-print coord. Fältskog was ecstatic about the video: "When I saw the video for the first time, I couldn't believe my eyes! It was so beautiful and so emotional. Everything was there, even my beloved dogs and the very first car I ever owned. It captured it all."

Elofsson provided more background on the creation of the A and A+ albums, explaining, "When we made the album A ten years ago, it was a bit of a reaction against EDM and the dance music that dominated the pop world at the time. We deliberately did something that was the complete opposite. Arranger Peter Nordahl crafted timeless, strong arrangements. As we've brought the songs into today's music landscape, we were all surprised by how well they still work. The songs have blossomed into the pop tracks they were at their core. Anton, who wasn't part of the project last time, comes from a different generation and brought entirely new rhythms to the mix."

Elofsson also emphasized the careful consideration he gave to the project, given Agnetha's iconic status: "Agnetha is not just any artist—she is an icon with a rich legacy. We really felt the pressure to create something great. We didn't want to damage anything for ABBA or Agnetha, given the reputation they've built over the years. I'm really happy to say that I think we pulled it off."

Anni-Frid Lyngstad (Frida) released her solo album Frida Ensam in 1975 while ABBA was still active. The album featured covers of popular songs such as David Bowie's "Life on Mars," 10cc's "Wall Street Shuffle," The Beach Boys' "Wouldn't It Be Nice," and Charlie Rich's "The Most Beautiful Girl in the World." It also included some Italian ballads. Most notably, the album featured the song "Fernando," originally written for this project. Thanks to Fernando, the album reached number one in Sweden. Frida explained her approach: "On the album, I included a lot of things I wanted to do but couldn't sing with ABBA because we're a group."

In 1982, Frida released her second solo album, Something's Going On, which marked a departure from ABBA's style. The lead single, "I Know There's Something Going On," written by Russ Ballard, closely resembled Phil Collins' hit "In the Air Tonight" from his Face Value album.

It sold three million copies worldwide. Frida reflected on the album's significance: "I thought the album's title was fitting because something was going on. From the time I started working on it, I felt a personal development beginning."

Her third album, Shine, was released under the Polar Music label and was produced by Steve Lillywhite. It included tracks like "Don't Do It," "That's Tough," a collaboration with her son Henrik Fredriksson and vocalist Kirsty MacColl, and "Slowly," written by Benny Andersson and Björn Ulvaeus. Frida expressed her satisfaction with this album: "The sound is bolder than on the last album. Steve helped open me up as a musician. Suddenly, I reached sounds and a way of working that I hadn't had an outlet for before—but now I've discovered it."

In 1996, Anni-Frid Lyngstad released the album Djupa andetag (Deep Breaths) in Scandinavia, which reached number one on the Sverigetopplistan chart. The album featured a variety of songs, including her self-penned track "Kvinnor Som Springer" (Women Who Run with the Wolves), as well as "Alla Mina Bästa År," "Ögonen," and "Även En Blomma." A documentary about the making of the album, featuring video clips and recordings from the production process, was aired on Sveriges Television. This documentary was also included in the DVD Frida—The DVD, which offered interviews with Frida and the album's producer, Anders Glenmark.

Chapter 8

Non-ABBA Musicals Developed or Co-Developed by Benny Andersson and Bjorn Ulvaeus

Benny Andersson and Björn Ulvaeus ventured into musical theater unrelated to ABBA music. They wrote the music for the musical Chess, with lyrics written by Tim Rice and Ulvaeus. Three of the songs in the musical that appeared on the Chess concept album hit the top 10—"One Night in Bangkok," "Nobody's Side," and "I Knew Him So Well." The play focused on a chess tournament between an American and Soviet grandmaster during the Cold War and their battle over a woman.

Benny Andersson and Björn Ulvaeus also created a musical called Kristina från Duvemåla (Kristina from Duvemåla) about Swedish immigrants to the US that opened in Malmö in October 1995. The musical was based on novels by Vilhelm Moberg. It opened in Minneapolis and Lindström in Minnesota in 1996 and was presented in Swedish. It was later staged in Gothenburg and Stockholm. The score spanned folk tunes, symphonies, and musical theater. Stany Van Wymeeersch describes the music for the musical Kristina as a more classical kind of music.

The play takes place in the 1840s and 1850s and recounts the plight of Kristina and her husband Karl Oskar, who are forced to leave their land in Småland, Sweden, "due to crop failures" and emigrate to the Lindström area in Minnesota. They face many challenges and hardships there but manage to endure despite those troubles, though up to a point. The original triple CD set was released in 1996 and peaked at number two on the Swedish album chart. It won the Swedish Grammis Award as best album in 1996. For a number of years, the song Guldet blev till Sand (Gold

Can Turn to Sand), performed by Peter Jöback (and written by Jöback and Benny Andersson), spent the longest amount of time on the national Swedish radio chart Svensktoppen."

Björn Ulvaeus and Herbert Kretzmer translated the show into English in the mid-2000s, and English-language productions appeared in the US and the UK subsequently.

Ulvaeus also wrote the lyrics for a circus musical called Pippi at the Circus based on a story from the highly popular Swedish children's book series called Pippi Longstocking written by Astrid Lindgren in the late 1960s. The musical opened in Stockholm in 2022. Benny Andersson wrote music for the show, and an album of the show was also released.

He also has ventured into classical music and released a solo music album called Piano in 2017 on the classical Deutsches Grammophon label. The album's 21 songs include songs from Chess, Kristina från Duvemåla, and material from his band Benny Andersson's Orchestra, as well as a version of "Thank You for the Music."

Chapter 9

ABBA Tribute Bands- Helping Carry the ABBA Flag Further

A whole industry of ABBA tribute bands has mushroomed over the last 35–40 years. In fact, according to the Ice 36 blog, ABBA is one of the most covered bands ever. ABBA tribute acts received over 65,000 searches between 2023 and 2024. As Madison Kim states, ABBA tribute bands, such as Abbaesque, A-Teens, Bjorn Again, and Gabba, have dedicated their efforts to spreading ABBA's legacy worldwide.

Their performances typically trigger instantaneous and exuberant audience participation—singing and dancing, seemingly on cue. Audience members even don costumes somewhat akin to those of the band. At the same time, the quality and authenticity of these bands vary considerably.

One of the most prominent ABBA tribute bands is Arrival from Sweden. Victoria Norback, the band's founder and show producer, says it was established by her in 1995 with ABBA's original bass player, Rutger Gunnarsson. She distinguishes the band from other ABBA tribute bands by "our respectful and serious attitude towards ABBA" and by the fact that "we have very talented musicians and play 100% live." She adds, "We tell a story about the band." As she observes, it's actually "very hard to play ABBA's music, though the music sounds simple." The band has utilized a number of musicians who played with ABBA, including "Mike Watson, a bass player, guitarist Janne Schaffer, and drummer Ola Bunkert." The varied backgrounds of the musicians add new dimensions to the ABBA music they play. For example, guitarist Daniel Palmqvist integrates more rock dynamics into some of the ABBA songs Arrival plays, and keyboardist Lalle Larsson comes from a "progressive rock" background.

Norback reports that Arrival's audience typically ranges in age from 40–80 in regular shows, and tends to be older in shows we perform with symphony orchestras, though she notes the shows are family-oriented. Depending on the venue and market, the band makes a point of playing lesser-known ABBA songs, such as "Waiting for You," "Tiger," and "Hey Helen," she says. She also reports that Arrival received "the right from ABBA to record their unreleased song 'Just a Notion' in 1999."

Chapter 10 - ABBA's Strong Fan Support System

Chapter 11
ABBA Forever?

ABBA's future seems to have no bounds or time limitations. They've forged ahead boldly into new horizons, but will their allure fade away? One never knows for sure, but the preponderance of evidence indicates the enormous difficulty of duplicating ABBA's unrivalled success and impact. The band was counted out before but kept surging back.

ABBA's career can be viewed as a progression of seasons or chapters. They started out as a bouncy pop group with accessible hits that transformed into multimedia co-packagers/entrepreneurs, developing new dimensions and outlets for their music. They've always grown organically and ventured forth on their own terms—for example, they waited for a very long time to release their expected last studio album, Voyage, in 2021.

ABBA is a unicorn. They've combined so many key elements at the right time and place that their unrivalled popularity with many diverse audiences would be extremely difficult to replicate in the future. The group helped pave the way for the worldwide success of many Swedish pop/rock groups and created a new paradigm for musical domination and branding.

The group marches on but in different ways. ABBA is firmly ensconced in the pantheon of pop music culture, and its iconic allure shows no signs of dissipating in the foreseeable future, especially with the popularity and expansion of its multimedia show Voyage, the inherently interactive nature of its music, and the many ABBA tribute bands that traverse the world playing their music.

Dr. Jadey O'Regan sums up ABBA's long-time appeal this way: "From their humble beginnings to global superstardom, ABBA 's music continues to resonate with audiences across generations, transcending cultural boundaries, and uniting listeners in a shared love for timeless melodies."

Writer and filmmaker Jaideep Varma singles out a key factor behind ABBA's enduring popularity: "During a time of enormous creativity and experimentation musically in pop music, there was a quiet sense of security to ABBA, who did not once set out to rebel fashionably against the status quo to be cool, get into drug-fuelled explorations, or try to be a musical entity they were not."

Anni-Frid Lyngstad paints a picture of the kind of legacy for ABBA she envisages: "I want the band to be remembered as a band who made people feel something in their hearts. I want to be remembered as a member of a band (of) people who gave them comfort, happiness, and the fact that we were there for them—and for ourselves as well, of course. I'm so happy that people are so touched by what we do."

The documentary ABBA: Against the Odds, which celebrates the 50th anniversary of the group's selection as winner of the Eurovision Song Contest, provides a long-term perspective on the group's career and its mark on pop music. The program aired on the BBC in April 2024 and offers access to Swedish Public TV archives, including rare footage that captures the band's rise to fame and the negativity they faced at home. ABBA didn't appear in the 50th Anniversary event in Sweden. The documentary was produced by James Rogan Productions, and James Rogan served as the director.

Rogan explains the tremendous impact of assembling the documentary on him and the enormity of ABBA's success: "To be able, as a director, to dive into the ABBA story through the extraordinary archive of their voyage through the tumultuous 70s has been a jaw-dropping experience. The sheer joy of working on a documentary about ABBA can't be understated, as their bittersweet songs remain as resonant in our confused times as they did when they were first recorded. This film will capture the scale of the challenge they faced as a Swedish band gaining success and respect on the global stage, and how the unique combination of four talents produced music that defined the decade and changed music forever."

Andersson looks back fondly on ABBA's work and his musical theater work, but also is at a loss to completely explain ABBA's long-term popularity. He said, "I don't understand why ABBA's music is still so popular. I hope it has something to do with the quality of the songs. We were really thorough. None of us would have thought when we quit in 1982 that our music would still be around 35 years on, but there is still as much life in those records as there was then. We were lucky. The music was kept alive by Muriel's Wedding, which was a really good film. Then Erasure recorded a few tracks and had a big success. Then ABBA Gold was re-released. And there must be millions of kids out there who don't know ABBA but know the songs from Mamma Mia! There are a lot of things that this young guy could have a reason to look forward to. I am very proud of what we achieved with ABBA, the music of Chess, and we also wrote a musical in Sweden called Kristina about Swedish immigration to North America in the 19th century. That was a huge success here—it is more of an opera, really."

Benny Andersson has given a sense of finality to ABBA's recording career with the declaration that they won't release any more albums after Voyage. He said, "I've said that's it. I don't want to do another ABBA album." Ulvaeus seems to feel similarly: "I never say never, but I agree with Benny. I think that was our goodbye." Although Anni-Frid Lyngstad doesn't hold out great hope for another album, she doesn't totally dismiss the possibility of more music from ABBA emerging: "Yeah, we have probably said it must be the last thing we do because, also thinking of our ages, we are not young any longer. But I would say again, you never know. So don't be too sure."

At the same time, Ulvaeus anticipates continuing to write music with Andersson. As he emphatically declares, he has no intention of retiring: "Would I rather potter in the garden? No, thank you. I'm a songwriter first and a music entrepreneur, I suppose, and I'll die with my boots on, definitely. I hope in some context or other, Benny and I would write a few more songs. I think there's much more in us. We can write for other people and other projects."

Andersson, for his part, doesn't foreclose the possibility of working with other acts, though he and Ulvaeus have never done so. As he puts it, "I would say I would take a look. We have been asked to do so, but we've never done it."

Finn Sjoberg doesn't believe there will be another ABBA, largely because "it took four talents that good" to play music at the highest level. As he puts it, "It's like with the Beatles. Can you imagine another Beatles?"

As Kenneth Patridge puts it, "ABBA's music is eternal."

According to Jaideep Varma, "There's little doubt ABBA's finest songs will last as long as the finest Beatles songs will."

Carl Magnus Palm doesn't believe there will ever be another ABBA. In his view, "They arrived at a time when the music business worked in a different way. ABBA's talents and skills were particular to that time."

Stany Van Wymeersh doesn't believe "there will be another band like ABBA. The band was part of a whole different system. ABBA created music that was very meaningful and poignant. They were very self-critical and perfectionists. Benny and Bjorn spent so much time on each track, and their music is unique. It's the same with the Beatles. All music now is commercialized and revolves around social media. Everyone now has access to everything in music production. But it's not possible in this world to create music like ABBA. Musicians are part of a different system now. Music today never reaches the emotional depth of ABBA's music, and a lot of pop music has a similar sound."

Capping off ABBA's storied career was the group's knighthood in May 2024 by King Carl Gustaf XVI and Queen Silvia, which was the first time the Swedish king had knighted any Swede in almost 50 years. They were given the Royal Order of Vasa "for outstanding efforts in Swedish and International pop music."

Bjorn Ulvaeus has often expressed amazement about the band's durability. He said, "It's very, very hard to grasp emotionally that we wrote these little songs, and it gave rise to this (the ABBA Voyage show) and the millions of people we have touched. We know it's true, but it's very hard to understand. Maybe impossible." He adds, "It's a very elusive feeling. It's more to do with gratitude and humility than pride, because it humbles you to know that so many people have listened to something you've created and that they've been made happy or sad, and that it has meant so much to them in their lives."

Jared Raab doesn't believe it's likely there will be another ABBA, as ABBA was so much a product of their time, and the world has changed completely. ABBA was too analog to duplicate now. It's hard to imagine another band duplicating their songwriting and success. At the same time, he admits, "History always surprises us."

What about further ABBA forays into new technology in the future? Ulvaeus is open to that idea: "There will be new exciting formats in the future we know very little about right now. AI, the metaverse, there are lots of interesting and exciting things happening creatively that ABBA might be involved in as well."

ABBA's music is so deeply embedded in the fabric of pop music that its influence will likely remain indelible, and its spell over the public will reign for the foreseeable future.

Whatever its future, ABBA's legacy is secure and resilient. They are firmly ensconced at the top of the pop elite, and they are sure to bring joy and wonderment to fans for many more years.

Appendix

Image Gallery

Set and costumes used in the first Mamma Mia! movie in ABBA Museum.

Glimpse of ABBA figures at ABBA Voyage Show (1)

Glimpse of ABBA figures at ABBA Voyage Show (2)

Agnetha Faltskog and Anni-Frid Lyngstad performing in Gothenburg in 1979

ABBA in "ABBA the Movie" (1)

ABBA in "ABBA the Movie" (2)

Poster of Abba the Movie

Poster of Abba the Movie

Mamma Mia! Here We Go Again Performance

Colin Firth, Pierce Brosnan, Benny Andersson, and Stellan Skarsgard on set of "Mamma Mia! Here We Go Again

Prince of Wales Theatre

Björn Ulvaeus

Meryl Streep in "Mamma Mia! Here We Go Again"

Björn Ulvaeus during Opening of ABBA- The Museum.

ABBA-The Museum.

ABBA Virtual figures in Signs for ABBA Voyage Show at West Ham United Olympic Stadium

ABBA-The Museum.

ABBA museum, Stockholm, Sweden

Arrival from Sweden, The Music of Abba (with permission from Swedtunes) (1)

Arrival from Sweden, The Music of Abba (with permission from Swedtunes) (2)

Concert of Arrival from Sweden- The Music of ABBA at Palanga concert hall, with permission from Swedtunes

ABBA Pinball Machine- Arrival Edition "with permission from Pinball Brothers."

ABBA Pinball Machine- Arrival Edition "with permission from Pinball Brothers."

ABBA Pinball Machine "with permission from Pinball Brothers."

ABBA Pinball Machine "with permission from Pinball Brothers."

The ABBA Fandom- An Online Survey" Conducted by ETOUR at Mid-Sweden University in 2019

Maria Lexhagen, Tatiana Chekalina, Christine Lundberg

Faculty of Human Sciences

ETOUR/Department of Business Economics, Law, Geography and Tourism

Mid Sweden University

Östersund, 2019-10-14

Printed by Mid Sweden University, Sundsvall

Faculty of Human Sciences

Mid Sweden University

Kunskapens väg 1

Phone: +46 (0)10 142 80 00

Report Series WP 2019:1

TABLE OF CONTENT

1 Introduction

Travel motives, engagement, social behavior and practices provide an interesting intersection for an investigation of the role of digital media in forming future behavior of fans travelling to places associated with popular culture such as music. Literature lacks empirical studies on music tourists and in particular the digital aspects of online practices. Therefore, the purpose of this study was to examine how digital media and online practices moderates the effect of involvement, social identity and motive on perceived value of tourist experiences and future travel behavior.

ABBA is a legendary pop music band from Sweden who had their last live performance in the 1980's. ABBA is highly associated with being from Sweden and it was therefore with great interest that ABBA fans received the news about the opening of ABBA the Museum in Stockholm in 2013. There is a big international fan community around ABBA even today and people who visit Sweden may have ABBA as a main or secondary motive for their trip. So far, there has not been any empirical scientific study of ABBA tourists in Sweden and therefore a main purpose of this study is to describe this group of tourists. There are two research questions for this study: 1) what is the ABBA tourists' profile and their respective online practices, and 2) what is the effect of social identity, involvement and travel motives on perceived value of ABBA tourism experiences as well as future interest in travelling, especially considering their online practices and experiences.

Further analysis on the empirical material of this study can be found in the publication of a book chapter; Lexhagen, M. (2018). Music fans as tourists: the mysterious ways of individual and social dimensions. In C. Lundberg and V. Ziakas (eds), *The Routledge Handbook on Popular Culture and Tourism*, Routledge, UK. Chapter 21, pp. 234-247.

2 Method

The results presented in this paper are based on an online survey of ABBA fans from 2013. The survey used a non-probabilistic snowball sampling and a link was available on the official ABBA fan club website, other ABBA fan club websites, ABBA-related Facebook groups, Twitter, and on ABBA the Museums Facebook page. The total number of respondents was 1 286.

The survey included questions about respondents' most recent ABBA-related trip such as visiting a location or destination associated with ABBA or participating in an event. It also included questions about their activities and previous experiences as an ABBA fan, information sources used, spending related to travel and purchasing ABBA products, web usage, future behavior, and background information (age, family situation, income, educational level, gender, and country of origin). Furthermore, questions on fan involvement, social identity, travel motives, social media use for ABBA-related trips, emotions related to web usage, and perceived value from ABBA related travel experiences, were included. The study employed a variety of univariate (proportions, medians and means), bivariate and multivariate analyses. The transformation of variables measured on an agreement scale was divided into two groups. Responses in the range from definitely disagree to neutral and in the range from somewhat to highly agree, was used as the grouping variables for in-depth analysis. Besides, categorization of numerical variables such as income and expenditures into four groups on the interquartile range basis was used to deal with the issue of extremely high values. Bivariate analysis include chi-square tests, t-tests and ANOVA, which was used to assess the differences between various groups of ABBA fans.

The cluster analysis performed in two steps assisted in classification of ABBA fans into segments based on a set of variables measured on a 7-point agreement scale. Examination of the agglomeration schedule and a dendogram as an output of hierarchical clustering (Ward's method, squared euqlidean distance) suggested the number of clusters. Consequently, K-means clustering classified the ABBA fans and helped evaluate the clusters' profiles and labeling. Cluster membership was then used as the grouping variable for bivariate analyses and significant differences between the clusters serve as evidence for cluster validity.

Finally, in order to empirically test the relationships between the offline and online fan involvement, social identity, web usage, web experience, travel motives, perceived value, social value, and future behavior intentions, the study utilized the structural equation modelling (SEM) technique by using the IBM SPSS AMOS (ver. 25).

2.1 Survey items for motives, social identity, and involvement

Table 2.1.1 Survey items motives

Motives measurement items 1= strongly disagree, 7= strongly agree	Developed from previous research
To experience a sense of belongingness to ABBA	Crompton, J. L. and McKay, S. L. (1997) 'Motives of visitors attending festival events', *Annals of Tourism Research*, 24: 426-39.
To experience a sense of belongingness to the ABBA community	Crompton, J. L. and McKay, S. L. (1997) 'Motives of visitors attending festival events', *Annals of Tourism Research*, 24: 426-39
To experience a "ABBA atmosphere"	Faulkner, B., Fredline, E. Larson, M. and Tomljenovic, R. (1999) 'A marketing analysis of Sweden's Storsjöyran musical festival', *Tourism Analysis*, 4:157-71.
To participate in activities that are fun	Formica, S. and Uysal, M. (1998) 'Market segmentation of an international cultural-historical event', *Journal of Travel Research*, 36: 16-24.
To experience new and different things	
To get away from the usual routine	Kim, N-S. and Chalip, L. (2004) 'Why travel to the FIFA World Cup? Effects of motives, background, interest, and constraints', *Tourism Management,* 25: 695-707.
To experience excitement	Mohr, K., Backman, K. E., Gahan, L. and Backman, S. J. (1993) 'An investigation of festival motivations and event satisfaction by visitor type', *Festival Management and Event Tourism*, 1: 89-98.
To party and drink	
To be with people who are enjoying themselves	Scott, D. (1996) 'A comparison of visitors' motivations to attend three urban festivals', *Festival Management and Event Tourism*, 3: 121-28.
To meet old friends	Smith, A.C.T. and Stewart, B. (2007) 'The travelling fan: understanding the mechanisms of sport fan consumption in a sport tourism setting', *Journal of Sport & Tourism*, 12: 155-81.
To meet new friends	Trail, G.T., and James, J.D. (2001) 'The motivation scale for sport consumption: Assessment of the
To share the experience with the people travelling with me	scale's psychometric properties', *Journal of Sport Behaviour*, 24: 108–27.
To have fun with my friends and/or family	Uysal, M., Backman, K., Backman, S. and Potts, T. (1991) 'An examination of event tourism motivations and activity', paper presented at New Horizons Conference, Calgary, Canada, July 1991.
To participate in other activities that are not ABBA related	Uysal, M., Gahan, L. and Martin, B. (1993) 'An examination of event motivations', *Festival Management and Event Tourism*, 1: 5-10.
To visit an attractive destination	Wann, D.L. (1995) 'Preliminary validation of the sport fan motivation scale', *Journal of Sport and Social Issues*, 19: 377–96.
To have an opportunity to visit this particular destination	*Authors' own*
	Authors' own
To watch people and be a part of the event/trip	*Authors' own*
	Authors' own
	Authors' own

Table 2.1.2. Survey items perceived value

Perceived value measurement items 1= strongly disagree, 7= strongly agree	Developed from previous research
The event/trip had a consistent quality	Babin, B. J., Darden, W. R. and Griffin, M. (1994) 'Work and/or fun: measuring hedonic and utilitarian shopping value', *Journal of Consumer Research*, 20: 644-56.
Relative to other events/trips I have participated at, this event/trip had an acceptable level of quality	
The result was expected	Overby, J. W. and Lee E-J. (2006) 'The effects of utilitarian and hedonic online shopping value on consumer preferences and intentions', *Journal of Business Research*, 59: 1160-66.
The event/trip exceeded my expectations	
The event/trip was a good purchase for the price paid	Petrick, J.F. (2002) 'Development of a multi-dimensional scale for measuring the perceived value of a service', *Journal of Leisure Research*, 34: 119-34.
The event/trip purchased was reasonably priced	Sánchez, J., Callrisa, L., Rodriguez R. M and Moliner, M. A. (2006) 'Perceived value of the purchase of a tourism product', *Tourism Management*, 27, 394-409.
The event/trip was well worth the time and effort spent	
The price was the main criterion for the decision	Steenkamp, J-B. E.M. and Geyskens, I. (2006) 'How Country characteristics affect perceived value of web sites', *Journal of Marketing*, 70: 136-50.
By participating at an ABBA related event/trip I accomplished just what I need	Sweeney, J. C. and Soutar G. N. (2001) 'Consumer perceived value: The development of a multiple item scale', *Journal of Retailing*, 77: 203-20.
I am comfortable with the event/trip I purchased	*Authors' own*
I enjoyed the event/trip	*Authors' own*
The event/trip made me feel good	*Authors' own*
During the event/trip I felt absorbed by the experience	*Authors' own*
	Authors' own
The event/trip was an escape	*Authors' own*
The event/trip gave me a chance to learn about new information and trends	*Authors' own*
	Authors' own
The event/trip made me excited	*Authors' own*
Compared to other things I could have done, the time and effort spent on this event/trip was truly enjoyable	*Authors' own*
	Authors' own
Participating at this event/trip helped me to feel acceptable	*Authors' own*
	Authors' own
This type of event/trip is taken by many people I know	*Authors' own*
	Authors' own
Participating at this event/trip improved the way I am perceived by others	*Authors' own*
	Authors' own
People who participate at this type of event/trip obtain social approval	*Authors' own*
I participated at this event/trip to make a good impression on other people	*Authors' own*
I participated at this event/trip to be able to interact and communicate with other people	

Table 2.1.3. Survey items social identity and involvement

Social identity and involvement items 1= strongly disagree, 7= strongly agree	Developed from previous research
Please evaluate the following statements as regards to your use of ABBA blogs/communities: My self-image overlaps with the identity of the user group as I perceive it When I'm interacting with other users on blogs/communities I feel there is an overlap between my personal identity and the identity of the group I am very attached to the user group I have a strong feeling of belongingness toward the user group I am a valuable member of the group I am an important member of the group	Social identity (Dholakia et al., 2004; Cheung et al., 2010) Item 1 and 2: cognitive social identity, item 3 and 4: affective social identity, item 5 and 6 evaluative social identity.
Please evaluate the following statements in relation to your involvement in ABBA: I'm interested in reading blogs about ABBA information and photos etc. When reading information in blogs I feel the information is appealing When reading information in blogs I feel that ABBA is relevant in my life When reading information in blogs I feel that ABBA means a lot to me I'm interested in ABBA ABBA is essential to me, thus it is difficult to choose between ABBA and my other hobbies Purchasing ABBA products is a ways of rewarding myself The ABBA products I purchase symbolize my personality and character I think ABBA blogs provide good efficiency in information searching I think ABBA blogs provide sufficient information I think what is written in ABBA blogs is reliable I think the communication in ABBA blogs is free from being interfered by sales-persons I think the communication in ABBA blogs is free from being interfered by friends outside the ABBA community	Involvement (Huang et al., (2010). Item 1-4: personal involvement, items 5-8: product involvement, items 9-13: situation involvement.

2.2 Other survey items

Table 2.2.1. Other survey items

Items	Scale
Background:	1= strongly disagree, 7= strongly agree
To what extent would you say you are an ABBA fan?	Numerical
How often do you listen to ABBA?	Numerical
If applicable, which year did you become an ABBA fan?	Numerical
How old were you when you became an ABBA fan?	Yes/No
Are you currently a paying member of the International ABBA Fan Club?	Yes/No
Do you plan to renew your membership when your subscription ends?	Online/Traditional media/Friends or family
Where do you get MOST of your news and information on ABBA?	Yes/No
Have you ever gone to see an ABBA tribute band play?	Yes/No
Do you have a collection of any ABBA memorabilia or merchandise? (i.e. something more than common albums and singles)	Name list
Do you own all of ABBA's albums?	Name list
Who is your favourite band member?	Numerical
Which band member's personality seems closest to yours?	Another continent/another country/another city/I haven't traveled beyond my hometown
How many ABBA concerts have you seen live? (i.e. not on TV, etc)	Yes/No
What is the farthest you've traveled to see ABBA live in concert?	Yes/No
Have you seen the musical Chess?	Yes/No
Have you seen the musical Kristina from Duvemala?	Yes/No
Have you ever traveled to Sweden due to its status as ABBA's birthplace?	Male/Female/Transsexual
Have you visited ABBA The Museum in Stockholm, Sweden?	Heterosexual/Homosexual/Bisexual
What is your gender?	Numerical
Sexual orientation?	Singel/Singel w children <18, married/partner, married/partner w children <18, other
Age?	Less than high school/High school/GED, some college, 2-year college degree, 4 year college degree, master's degree, doctoral degree, professional degree
Family?	List of all countries in the world
What is the highest level of education you have completed?	12 categories ranging from less than $10 000 to more than $150 000
Country of origin?	Yes/No
	Yes/No
	Numerical
	Numerical
	Numerical
	Numerical

Annual household income (before tax in US dollars)?	Numerical
	Numerical
Travel behavior	Agency or organization/online group or community/me, my family or close friends/other
Have you traveled or participated in events due to your interest in ABBA OTHER than ABBA The Museum (e.g. attended album releases, conventions or get-togethers, visited locations associated with ABBA, etc.)?	Name the destination you visited
	List of years from 1970-2013, list of months
	Yes/No
Have you ever traveled farther than 100 kilometers (62 miles) to participate in an ABBA related event/trip?	1-14 days or more
	Car/train/bus/airplane/boat/other
How many ABBA related events/trips have you participated in (total number), where ABBA was the PRIMARY motive for your participation?	Family/Real life friends/Family and friends/online friends/online and real life friends/by myself/other
How many of these (total number) were domestic?	Travel operator or agency online and offline/Social media/ABBA related websites/other websites/other ABBA related sources/Word-of-mouth in real life/Other
How many of these (total number) were international?	
	Open numerical
How many ABBA related events/trips have you participated in (total number), where ABBA was a SECONDARY motive for your participation?	Open numerical
	Yes/No
How many of these (total number) were domestic?	1=Not at all, 7=to a large extent
How many of these (total number) were international?	1=Not at all, 7=to a large extent
	1=Not at all, 7=to a large extent
Who organized these events/trips?	1=Not at all, 7=to a large extent
Regarding your most recent trip/event: Where did it take place and was your interest in ABBA a primary or secondary motive for this trip/event? Regarding your most recent trip/event: In what year and month did you take it?:	Several times a day/Every day/a few times every week/once every week/a few times every month/once every month less than every month/less than every six months/never
	Open numerical
Regarding your most recent trip/event: Would you at the time have traveled to this destination if it was not for ABBA?:	To find information on events and trips/to plan participation at events and trips/To book participation at events and trips/To find general information/To find information on the band members/To purchase ABBA related products/To read or watch ABBA related content/To find exclusive ABBA content/To look or download ABBA related pictures and applications/To watch or download fan-made videos/To interact with other fans/Other
Regarding your most recent trip/event: How many days was it? :	
Regarding your most recent trip/event: What was the primary mode of transportation to the destination?:	
Regarding your most recent trip/event: Who did you travel with?:	1-7 scale for; Unhappy/Happy; Annoyed/Pleased; Not contented/Contented; Despairing/Hopeful; Relaxed/Stimulated; Unaroused/Aroused; Sluggish/Frenzied; Calm/Excited; Sleepy/Wide awake
Regarding your most recent trip/event: What was your PRIMARY source of information when planning your event/trip?:	(Semantic differential scale. Coan, James A. & Allen, John, J. B., 2007)
Regarding your most recent trip/event: How much did you approximately spend in total (in US dollars)?:	
Regarding your most recent trip/event: How much would you be willing to spend for a similar experience in the future (in US dollars)?:	
Regarding your most recent trip/event: Did you pay to participate in a packaged event/trip/tour? If yes, please name the organizer(s).:	

Online behavior I have used information in blogs/communities to plan my participation Information in blogs/communities influenced my decision to participate Information in blogs/communities was helpful while I participated After I participated, I have shared my experiences on blogs/communities How often, on average, do you visit an ABBA related website/blog/community? Which year did you first start searching for ABBA related content on the Internet? When searching for ABBA related content on the Internet, which are your THREE main purposes? *Online experience* If you visit ABBA blogs/communities, to what extent do you agree with the following statement: "The blog/community where I found the link to this survey makes me feel..."	84

3 Findings

3.1 The ABBA fan sample background

In this study, 58.3% were men, 41.6% women and 0.1 transsexual. In terms of age, the respondents were between 16-65< where the majority, 58%, were 45-55 and 23% were 35-44 (fig. 3.1).

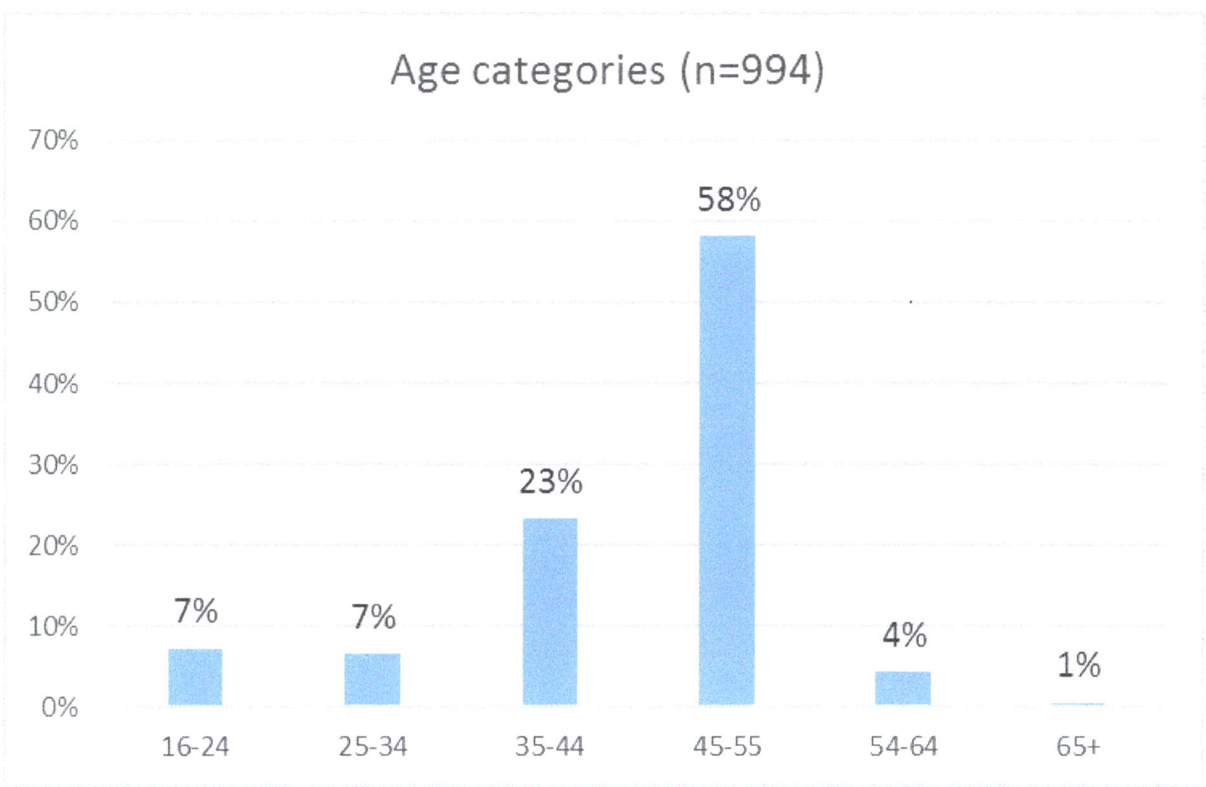

Figure 3.1. The ABBA fan sample age distribution

The survey respondents were from 58 different countries around the world, but mainly United Kingdom, 17.6%, Netherlands, 11.7%, and Germany, 11% (fig. 3.2). Nearly half of them were singles with or without children, 44.5%, followed by 26.2% who were in a relationship without children under 18 and 15.4% were in a relationship with children under 18. In terms of sexual orientation, 59% state a heterosexual orientation, while 36.2% state a homosexual or 4.8% bi-sexual orientation.

The results show that the respondents to a large degree regard themselves as a fan of ABBA (mean 6.5 on a scale of 1-7) (table 3.1). They listen to ABBA mostly every day or between 1-6 times a week and most of them became fans when ABBA was still actively recording and performing. However, a number of respondents indicated they have become fans of ABBA at a later or much later date. The absolute majority became fans at the age between under 12 years of age and up to 19 year of age.

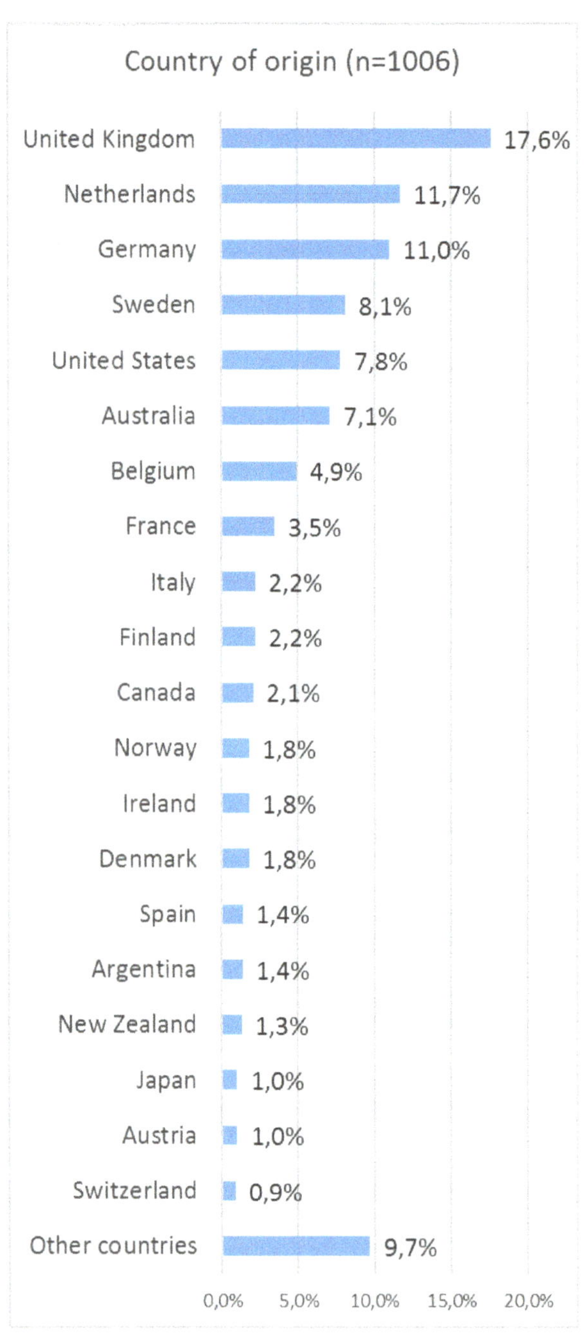

Figure 3.2. The country of origin

The results demonstrate a strong interest by respondents in ABBA since more than 80% own all of ABBAs albums, more than 75% have ABBA memorabilia or merchandise, 34% are currently members of the international ABBA fan club and 32% have visited the ABBA museum in Stockholm, but 77% have not seen a live ABBA concert. In terms of travel, 51% have travelled to Sweden due to its association to ABBA and 86% have travelled based on their interest in ABBA. 37% of those who had ABBA as the primary motive for travel (with 19% taking international trips) have travelled more than 10 times and 62% between 1 and 10 times.

Table 3.1. Fan involvement and social identity (1 – strongly disagree, 7 – strongly agree)

Variable	N	Mean	Std. Dev.
Offline fan involvement - interest in ABBA			
To what extent would you say you are an ABBA fan?	921	6,5	1,110
I'm interested in ABBA	1223	6,5	1,141
I feel that ABBA is essential to me, therefore I prioritize ABBA over my other hobbies	1217	4,6	1,909
Purchasing ABBA products is a way of rewarding myself	1219	4,6	2,047
The ABBA products I purchase symbolize my personality and character	1221	4,3	2,061
Online involvement - interest in ABBA and social media usage			
I'm interested in reading information and seeing photos of ABBA in blogs/communities	976	5,8	1,622
When reading information in blogs/communities I feel that ABBA means a lot to me	966	5,1	1,883
I think ABBA blogs/communities provide good efficiency in information searching	964	5,0	1,747
When reading information in blogs/communities I feel the information is appealing	962	5,0	1,669
I think ABBA blogs/communities provide sufficient information	963	4,9	1,685
When reading information in blogs/communities I feel that ABBA is relevant in my life	971	4,8	1,904
I think the communication in ABBA blogs/communities is free from being interfered by friends outside the ABBA community	959	4,5	1,761
I think the communication in ABBA blogs/communities is free from being interfered by sales-persons	957	4,5	1,781
I think what is written in ABBA blogs/communities is reliable	960	4,4	1,674
Social identity - Use of ABBA blogs/communities			
My self-image fits with the identity of the community	962	3,5	1,946
When I'm interacting with the community my personal identity is strengthened	957	3,2	1,927
I have a strong feeling of belonging toward the user group	950	3,1	1,935
I am very attached to the user group	946	2,9	1,889
I am a valuable member of the group	951	2,9	1,919
I am an important member of the group	950	2,7	1,899

In addition, ABBA fan involvement is manifested through various ABBA related activities such as: 1) membership in the international ABBA fan club, 2) ownership of all ABBA albums and an ABBA memorabilia collection, 3) attendance of ABBA tribute band concerts, musicals and other ABBA-related events, 4) travelling for the purpose of attending an ABBA related event, 5) travelling to Sweden due to its status as ABBA's birthplace and, 6) visiting ABBA The Museum in Stockholm, Sweden (table 3.2).

Table 3.2. Involvement in various ABBA-related activities

Variable	N	%
Are you currently a paying member of the International ABBA Fan Club?	1220	33,9%
Do you own all of ABBA's albums?	1204	84,8%
Do you have a collection of any ABBA memorabilia or merchandise? (i.e. something more than common albums and singles)	1206	76,8%
Have you ever gone to see an ABBA tribute band play?	1212	63,5%
Have you seen the musical Chess?	1199	50,1%
Have you seen the musical Kristina from Duvemala?	1196	25,7%
Have you visited ABBA The Museum in Stockholm, Sweden?	849	32,3%
Have you ever traveled to Sweden due to its status as ABBA's birthplace?	1194	50,7%
Have you ever traveled farther than 100 kilometers (62 miles) to participate in an ABBA related event/trip?	634	85,8%
Have you traveled or participated in events due to your interest in ABBA OTHER than ABBA The Museum (e.g. attended album releases, conventions or get-togethers, visited locations associated with ABBA, etc.)?	1147	55,1%

The involvement in various ABBA-related activities has been summarized as an index ranging from 0 to 10 (fig. 3.3).

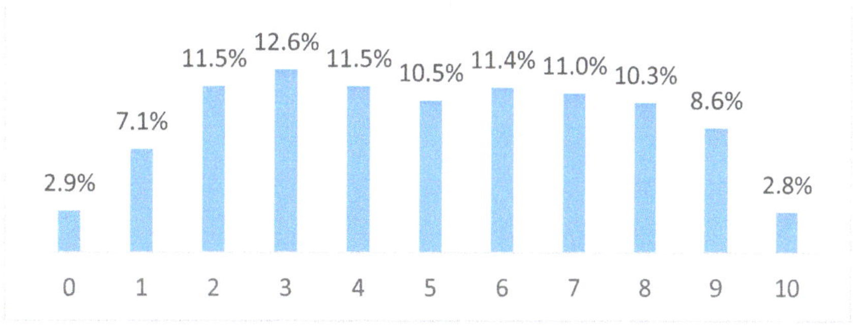

Figure 3.3. Fan involvement index (n=1222)

89

For the majority of the respondents, their most recent trip lasted 4-7 days (fig. 3.4) and they travelled mostly with real life friends or family. However, 27% travelled by themselves, and slightly more than 5% travelled with online friends or real-life and online friends (fig. 3.5).

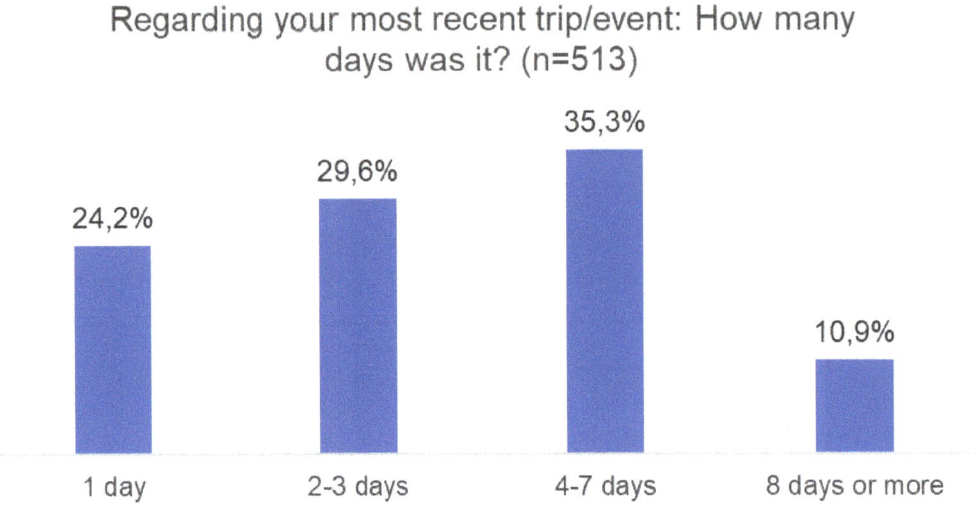

Figure 3.4. Duration of ABBA related trip/event

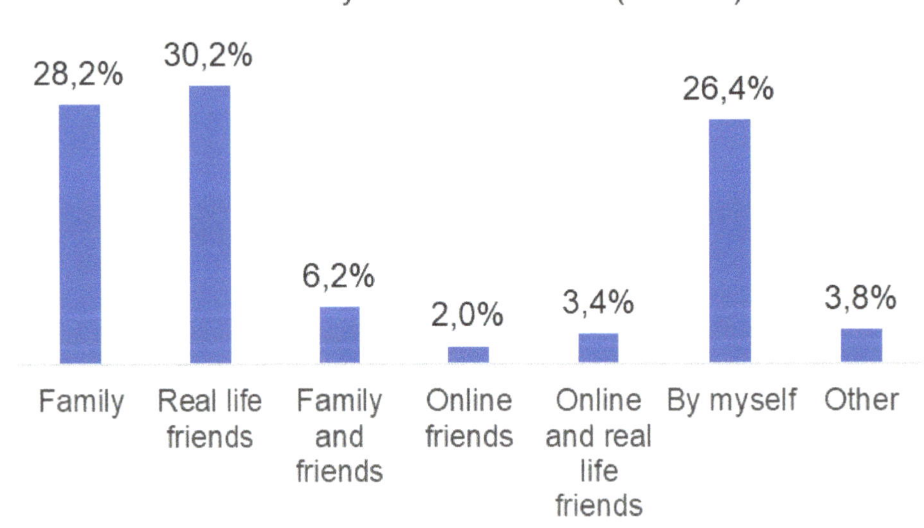

Figure 3.5. Travel/event participation accompaniment

Their primary source of information prior to the trip was ABBA related websites, followed by other websites, social media, travel operator/travel agency, other ABBA-related sources, and offline word-of-mouth (fig. 3.6).

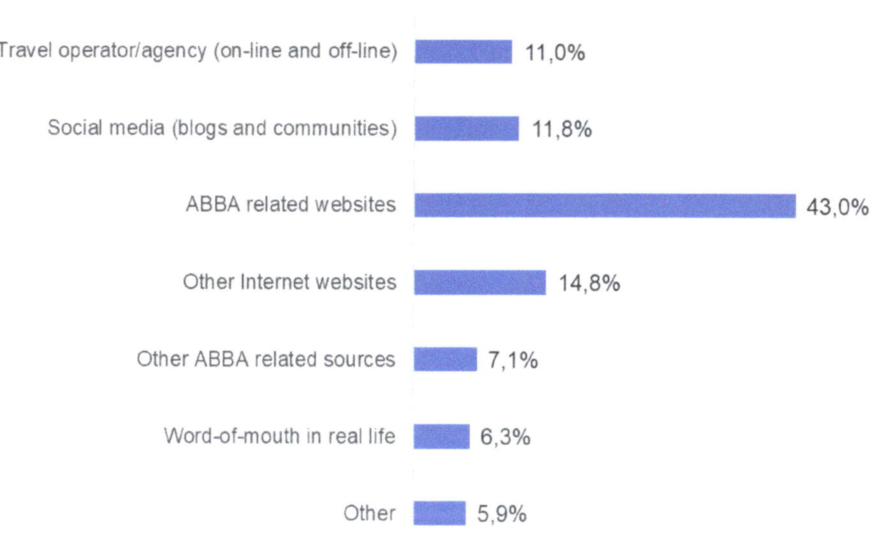

Figure 3.6. The information sources prior to ABBA-related trip/event

The maximum expenditure for the trip or event was $35,000 but the majority (i.e., 75%) spent up to $1,000 (median $500) (fig. 3.7).

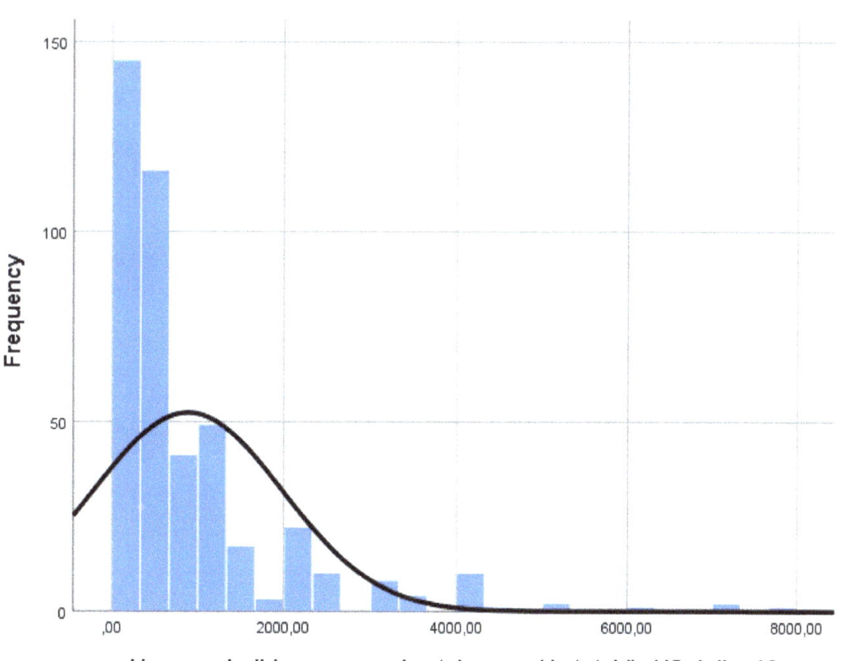

Figure 3.7. Expenditures in connection to ABBA-related trip/event

Fans have also stated that they are interested in participating in ABBA-related travel in the future (mean of 5.4 on a scale from 1-7) and to recommend others to do so (mean 5). Adding to this, they have also to some extent shared their experiences after traveling in blogs and communities (mean 4.1).

Online fan practices are evident and 66.3% visited ABBA-related websites, blogs or communities from several times a day to a few times every week (fig. 3.8).

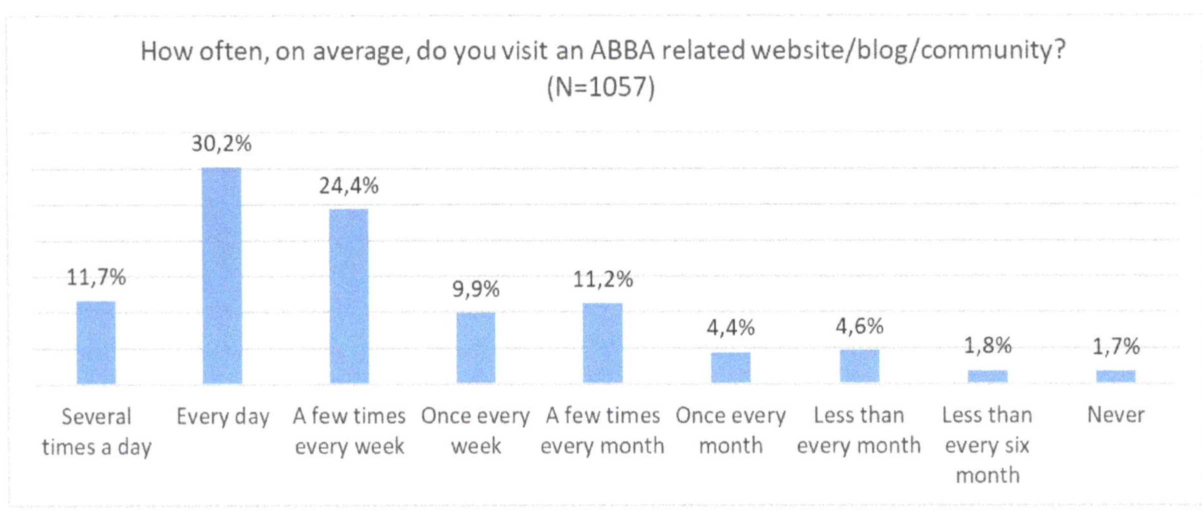

Figure 3.8. Average ABBA-related web usage

The most commonly mentioned reasons, in order of importance, for being online is to 1) find information about band members, 2) to read or watch ABBA-related content, 3) to find information in general about ABBA, 4) to purchase ABBA-related product, 5) to find exclusive content, or 6) interact with other fans (fig. 3.9). The emotional experiences of visiting ABBA blogs and communities mostly center on feeling happy, pleased and contented, as well as somewhat excited, aroused and frenzied (table 3.3).

Table 3.3. Emotional experience of visiting ABBA blogs and communities (If you visit ABBA blogs/communities, to what extent do you agree with the following statement: "The blog/community where I found the link to this survey makes me feel"; 1-7)

Variable	N	Mean	Std. Dev.
Unhappy - Happy	900	5,7	1,381
Annoyed - Pleased	880	5,5	1,488
Not contented- Contented	857	5,3	1,471
Calm - Excited	860	4,8	1,648
Unaroused - Aroused	838	4,3	1,705
Sluggish - Frenzied	831	4,3	1,569

On a scale from 1-7 the results show that fans have used blogs and communities to plan their participation in ABBA-related travel (mean 4.9) and that the information they found influenced their decision to participate (mean 4.1).

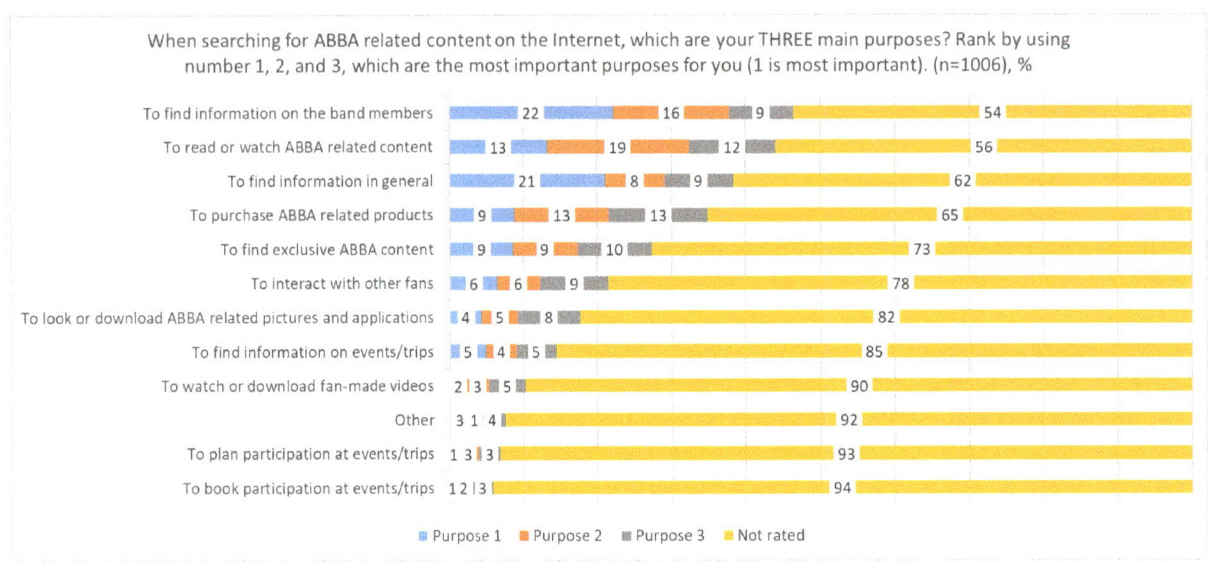

Figure 3.9. Reasons for being online

3.2 ABBA fan segmentation based on fan involvement and social identity

Examination of descriptive analysis results suggested that ABBA fans do not constitute a homogeneous group. This result is coherent in particular with leisure research studies on involvement where Havitz and Dimanche (144) propose the use of segmentation in order to capture the various facets of how involvement influences behavior. Hence, a cluster analysis was used to categorize ABBA fans into sub-groups and identified three distinct ABBA fan-segments related to involvement and perceptions of social identity among fans: (1) interested non-devoted; (2) hooked independent; and (3) eager-enthusiastic-group-member (table 3.4).

Table 3.4. Fan identity and involvement cluster membership

Variable	1 – Interested non-devoted		2 – Hooked independent		3 – Eager enthusiastic group member		Sig.
	N	Mean	N	Mean	N	Mean	
To what extent would you say you are an ABBA fan?	269	5,9	356	6,6	296	6,9	<0.001
I'm interested in ABBA	331	5,9	508	6,7	384	6,9	<0.001
I feel that ABBA is essential to me, therefore I prioritize ABBA over my other hobbies	329	2,9	504	4,7	384	6,0	<0.001
Purchasing ABBA products is a way of rewarding myself	330	2,5	505	4,8	384	6,1	<0.001
The ABBA products I purchase symbolize my personality and character	328	2,4	507	4,3	386	6,0	<0.001
I'm interested in reading information and seeing photos of ABBA in blogs/communities	232	4,2	435	6,1	309	6,7	<0.001
When reading information in blogs/communities I feel the information is appealing	226	3,1	431	5,2	305	6,2	<0.001
When reading information in blogs/communities I feel that ABBA is relevant in my life	230	2,4	433	5,1	308	6,3	<0.001
When reading information in blogs/communities I feel that ABBA means a lot to me	230	2,7	429	5,5	307	6,5	<0.001
I think ABBA blogs/communities provide good efficiency in information searching	231	3,0	430	5,3	303	6,3	<0.001
I think ABBA blogs/communities provide sufficient information	232	3,1	427	5,1	304	6,1	<0.001
I think what is written in ABBA blogs/communities is reliable	230	2,8	424	4,4	306	5,6	<0.001
I think the communication in ABBA blogs/communities is free from being interfered by sales-persons	228	2,9	426	4,5	303	5,6	<0.001
I think the communication in ABBA blogs/communities is free from being interfered by friends outside the ABBA com	227	2,9	430	4,5	302	5,7	<0.001
My self-image fits with the identity of the community	229	1,9	431	3,1	302	5,3	<0.001
When I'm interacting with the community my personal identity is strengthened	226	1,7	430	2,7	301	5,1	<0.001

I am very attached to the user group	225	1,5	424	2,2	297	5,0	<0.001
I have a strong feeling of belonging toward the user group	226	1,5	428	2,4	296	5,2	<0.001
I am a valuable member of the group	227	1,5	428	2,2	296	5,0	<0.001
I am an important member of the group	227	1,4	427	2,0	296	4,8	<0.001

The interested non-devoted group, the smallest group, have a generally low level of involvement and social identity but still with a high level of general interest in ABBA. They express this as an interest in ABBA and they actually label themselves as ABBA fans.

The hooked independent group, the largest segment, are more involved in their ABBA interest, where they prioritize their interest over other things and purchase ABBA-related products as a reward or symbol of their personality and character. They are also more involved and interested in online information and interaction, especially in terms of looking for information that is appealing, relevant and meaningful on a personal level, is an efficient way of finding information, and represents a place that is not interfered by people outside the ABBA community. However, they have low scores for all measures on social identity, implying they do not have a sense of attachment, belongingness, membership or sense of fit between self-image and identity of the community. At the same time, they also identify themselves as an ABBA fan.

The group of fans who belong to the eager-enthusiastic-group-member segment identify themselves as an ABBA fan, have high scores for both involvement, on- and offline, as well as social identity. They are highly involved with their interest in ABBA, their online activities as well as experience support a sense of fit between their own self and the group identity. Especially those ABBA fans travelling together with their online friends, as well as fans who attended more than 10 ABBA related events or trips view themselves as valuable members of the online ABBA community (i.e., social identity).

Remarkably, the eager fans segment has much more singles with or without children (62.5) than those who are married or live in a common law relationships (37.5), while the proportion of singles and couples is relatively even among other two segments (fig. 3.10).

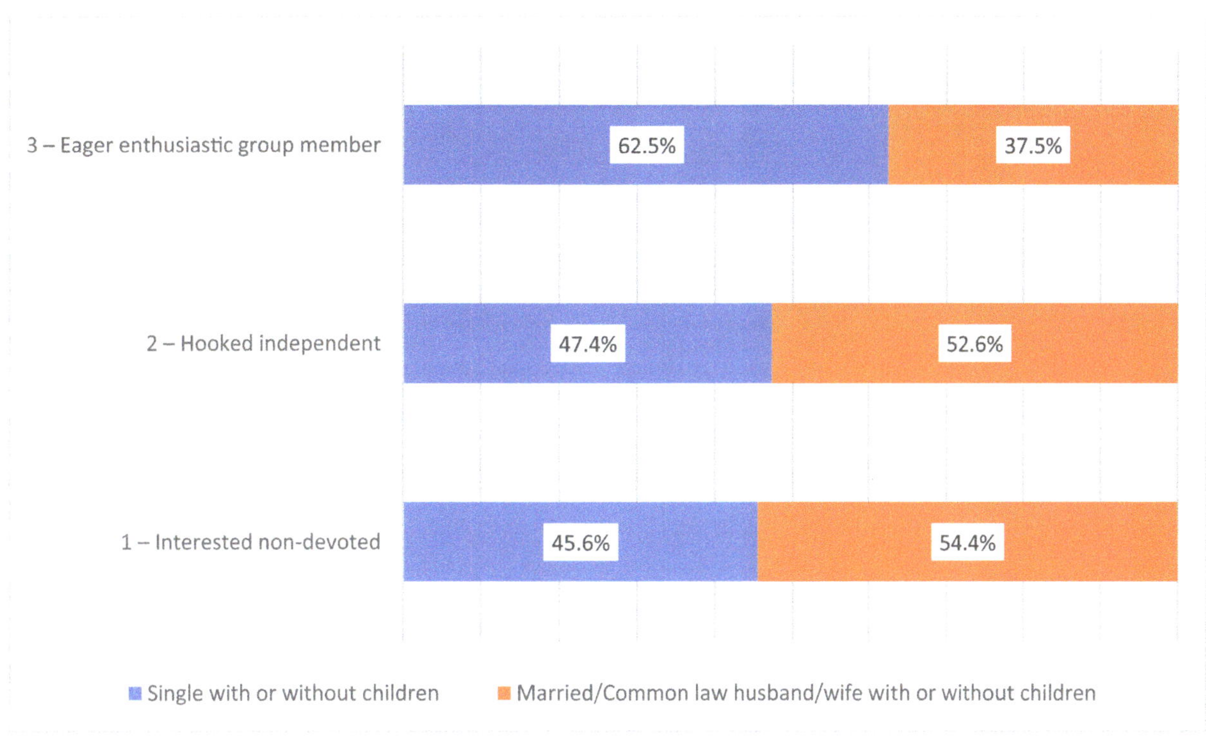

Figure 3.10. Relationship status (sig. <0.001)

It is also interesting that singles are significantly more interested in purchasing ABBA merchandise, reading and showing more trust in blogs and communities, and score higher on all indicators of social identity (table 3.5).

Table 3.5. Comparison of offline and online fan involvement and social identity based on relationship status (1-7)

Variable	Singles	Couples	Sig.
I'm interested in reading information and seeing photos of ABBA in blogs/communities	5,8	5,9	n.s.
I'm interested in ABBA	6,6	6,6	n.s.
I feel that ABBA is essential to me, therefore I prioritize ABBA over my other hobbies	4,8	4,5	*
Purchasing ABBA products is a way of rewarding myself	4,9	4,5	**
The ABBA products I purchase symbolize my personality and character	4,6	4,1	***
To what extent would you say you are an ABBA fan?	6,6	6,5	n.s.
When reading information in blogs/communities I feel the information is appealing	5,2	4,9	**
When reading information in blogs/communities I feel that ABBA is relevant in my life	5,0	4,6	***
When reading information in blogs/communities I feel that ABBA means a lot to me	5,3	4,9	**
I think ABBA blogs/communities provide good efficiency in information searching	5,2	4,9	n.s.
I think ABBA blogs/communities provide sufficient information	5,0	4,8	n.s.
I think what is written in ABBA blogs/communities is reliable	4,6	4,2	***
I think the communication in ABBA blogs/communities is free from being interfered by sales-persons	4,6	4,2	**
I think the communication in ABBA blogs/communities is free from being interfered by friends outside the ABBA com	4,7	4,2	***
My self-image fits with the identity of the community	3,8	3,3	***
When I'm interacting with the community my personal identity is strengthened	3,5	3,0	***
I am very attached to the user group	3,2	2,7	**
I have a strong feeling of belonging toward the user group	3,4	2,8	***
I am a valuable member of the group	3,2	2,6	***
I am an important member of the group	3,0	2,5	***

Significance level (t-test): *** (<0.001), ** (<0.01), * (<0.1)

The group of eager-enthusiastic-group-member fans has a significantly lower income level compared to the other two fan segments, as 62% of this group, 49% of hooked independents and 47% interested non-devoted fans reported income below $50,000 (fig. 3.11).

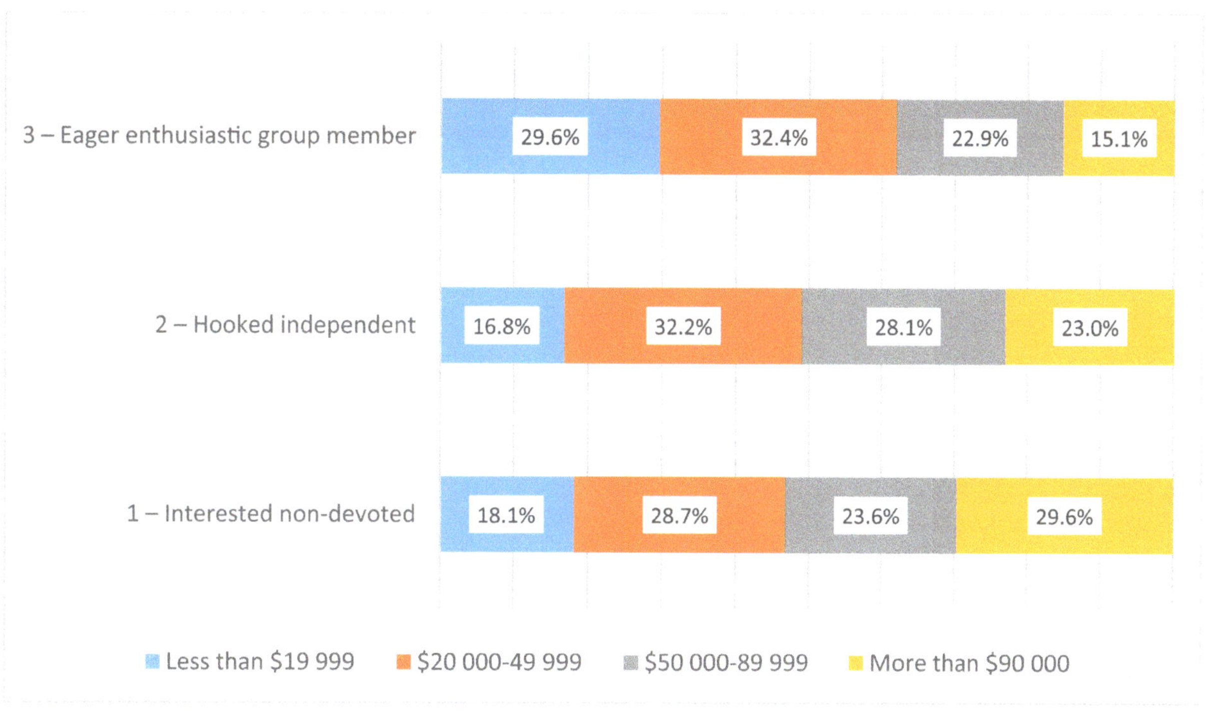

Figure 3.11. Income (sig. <0.001)

Fans with income below $20,000 have the highest online and off-line involvement and social identity scores and fans with income above $90,000 have the lowest (table 3.6).

Table 3.6. Comparison of offline and online fan involvement and social identity based on the income level (1-7)

Variables	Less than $19 999	$20 000-49 999	$50 000-89 999	Over $90000	Sig.
To what extent would you say you are an ABBA fan?	6,6	6,6	6,5	6,5	n.s.
I'm interested in ABBA	6,7	6,6	6,6	6,5	n.s.
I feel that ABBA is essential to me, therefore I prioritize ABBA over my other hobbies	5,3	4,7	4,7	4,3	***
Purchasing ABBA products is a way of rewarding myself	5,0	4,7	4,7	4,4	*
The ABBA products I purchase symbolize my personality and character	4,8	4,5	4,3	4,1	**
I'm interested in reading information and seeing photos of ABBA in blogs/communities	6,2	5,8	5,8	5,8	*
When reading information in blogs/communities I feel the information is appealing	5,4	5,1	4,9	4,8	**
When reading information in blogs/communities I feel that ABBA is relevant in my life	5,4	4,9	4,7	4,6	***
When reading information in blogs/communities I feel that ABBA means a lot to me	5,6	5,2	5,1	4,8	**
I think ABBA blogs/communities provide good efficiency in information searching	5,4	5,1	5,0	4,8	*
I think ABBA blogs/communities provide sufficient information	5,3	4,9	4,9	4,7	**
I think what is written in ABBA blogs/communities is reliable	4,9	4,5	4,4	4,0	***
I think the communication in ABBA blogs/communities is free from being interfered by sales-persons	4,8	4,5	4,5	4,2	**
I think the communication in ABBA blogs/communities is free from being interfered by friends outside the ABBA com	4,9	4,5	4,5	4,3	*
My self-image fits with the identity of the community	3,9	3,6	3,6	3,1	***
When I'm interacting with the community my personal identity is strengthened	3,7	3,3	3,3	2,7	***
I am very attached to the user group	3,4	3,0	3,0	2,6	***

I have a strong feeling of belonging toward the user group	3,7	3,1	3,1	2,7	***
I am a valuable member of the group	3,3	3,0	2,9	2,5	***
I am an important member of the group	3,1	2,9	2,7	2,3	***

Significance level (ANOVA): *** (<0.001), ** (<0.01), * (<0.1)

Income goes hand in hand with price sensitivity, as 38% of eager fans, 22% of hooked independent fans and only 10% of interested non-devoted fans agreed with the statement that the price was the main criterion for the decision to participate in ABBA-related trips and events.

3.3 Motivation-based segmentation of ABBA fans

A cluster analysis was also used to group fans with respect to types of motives for ABBA-related travel and participation in ABBA events: (1) highly motivated; (2) shillyshallies; (3) get-togethers; (4) thrill seekers; and (5) emotional junkies (table 3.7). The highly motivated group of fans, which is also the biggest segment, have high scores for all types of motives, which means they are motivated by ABBA specific things like belonging to an ABBA community, belongingness with ABBA, and an ABBA atmosphere, and participating in ABBA-related activities. Nevertheless, other traditional types of tourism motives are also important for this group, such as being with friends and family, having fun and enjoying themselves, experiencing new, exciting and different things, getting away, or visit an attractive or particular destination. The shillyshallies, the smallest segment, mostly have low scores and scattered across all types of motives without any distinct pattern. The third segment, the get-togethers (equal in size with segment four and five), focus on social aspects. Experiencing an ABBA atmosphere, meeting old friends, and having fun with friends and family are typical motives.

Table 3.7. Motivation-based cluster membership

Variables	Highly motivated		Shillyshallies		Get-togethers		Thrill seekers		Emotion junkies		Total		Sig.
	N	Mean	N	Mean	N	Mean	N	Mean	N	Mean	N	Mean	
To experience a sense of belonging to ABBA	181	6,0	51	3,3	82	4,8	85	3,7	80	6,5	479	5,2	<0.000
To experience a sense of belonging to the ABBA community	181	6,1	49	2,9	83	4,8	85	2,8	80	6,1	478	4,9	<0.000
To experience an "ABBA atmosphere"	182	6,6	50	4,2	83	5,5	85	5,1	80	6,6	480	5,9	<0.000
To participate in activities that are fun	181	6,6	49	3,8	81	5,5	84	5,5	80	6,1	475	5,8	<0.000
To experience new and different things	180	6,3	49	3,3	83	4,0	85	5,8	79	5,8	476	5,4	<0.000
To get away from the usual routine	180	6,2	48	2,5	82	3,6	85	5,2	79	4,6	474	4,9	<0.000
To experience excitement	179	6,6	49	2,9	82	4,4	83	5,6	80	5,8	473	5,6	<0.000
To party and drink	179	4,7	49	1,9	83	3,0	85	2,6	77	2,1	473	3,3	<0.000
To be with people who are enjoying themselves	180	6,3	50	2,3	82	4,9	85	4,0	79	4,0	476	4,9	<0.000
To meet old friends	180	5,8	50	2,6	83	5,6	85	2,2	80	2,4	478	4,2	<0.000
To meet new friends	180	5,8	48	2,2	81	4,5	85	2,7	79	3,3	473	4,3	<0.000
To share the experience with the people traveling with me	177	6,2	49	1,9	83	5,0	82	4,9	79	3,5	470	4,8	<0.000
To have fun with my friends and/or family	178	6,5	49	3,0	83	5,7	85	5,1	79	3,8	474	5,3	<0.000
To participate in other activities that are not ABBA related	180	5,2	50	2,2	82	3,9	84	5,3	79	2,4	475	4,2	<0.000
To visit an attractive destination	180	5,9	49	2,5	80	4,5	85	6,3	78	3,5	472	5,0	<0.000
To visit this particular destination	179	6,0	49	3,0	81	4,8	85	6,3	78	4,3	472	5,2	<0.000
To watch people and be a part of the event/trip	179	6,0	49	2,1	82	4,5	84	3,9	79	3,9	473	4,6	<0.000

Significance level (ANOVA): *** (<0.001), ** (<0.01), * (<0.1)

The fourth segment, the thrill seekers, are different in that they focus more on traditional tourism type motives such as fun and excitement, experiencing new and different things, and visiting an attractive or particular destination. Finally, the emotional junkies group of fans have high scores for motives related to an ABBA atmosphere, belonging to ABBA and the ABBA community in combination with fun and excitement and experiencing new and different things.

Among the five segments, the group of highly motivated fans has the highest scores on all aspects of fan involvement such as interest in merchandise and engagement with the online community, as well as on social identity with the fan community (table 3.8).

The highly motivated fans group is also the dominating segment within the eager-enthusiastic-group-member segment implying that the highly motivated in fact overlap (60%) with the fan segment where fans identify themselves as fans of ABBA and who have a strong sense of social identity with the community and engage a lot in online practices (fig. 3.12).

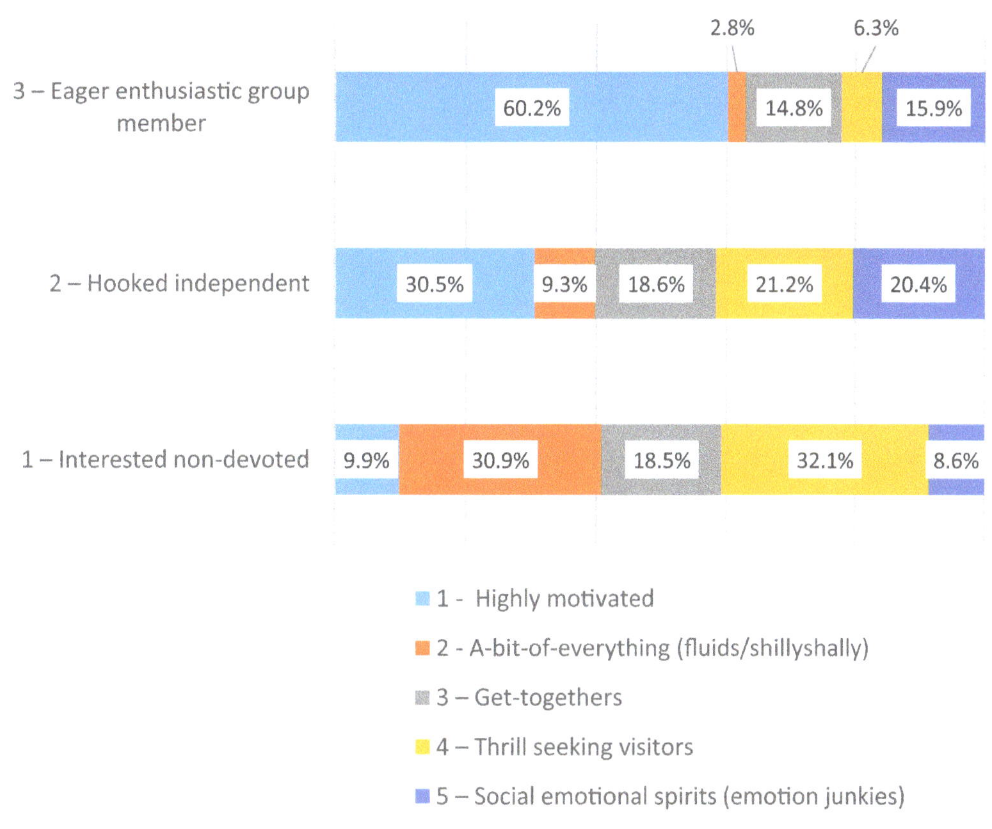

Figure 3.12. Representation of motivation cluster membership within fan involvement and social identity clusters (sig. <0.001)

Table 3.8. Comparison of offline and online fan involvement and social identity based on motivation cluster membership (1-7), sig. <0.001

Variables	Highly motivated	Shillyshallies	Get-togethers	Thrill seekers	Emotion junkies
To what extent would you say you are an ABBA fan?	6,9	5,8	6,5	6,6	6,9
I'm interested in ABBA	6,9	6,0	6,6	6,6	6,9
I feel that ABBA is essential to me, therefore I prioritize ABBA over my other hobbies	5,7	3,6	5,2	4,3	5,5
Purchasing ABBA products is a way of rewarding myself	5,8	3,4	4,6	4,5	5,3
The ABBA products I purchase symbolize my personality and character	5,4	2,9	3,7	3,9	5,1
I'm interested in reading information and seeing photos of ABBA in blogs/communities	6,5	4,9	5,9	5,5	6,3
When reading information in blogs/communities I feel the information is appealing	5,7	4,0	5,0	4,6	5,5
When reading information in blogs/communities I feel that ABBA is relevant in my life	5,7	3,7	4,7	4,3	5,5
When reading information in blogs/communities I feel that ABBA means a lot to me	6,0	3,8	5,1	4,6	5,8
I think ABBA blogs/communities provide good efficiency in information searching	5,9	4,1	5,1	4,5	5,7
I think ABBA blogs/communities provide sufficient information	5,6	4,1	4,9	4,3	5,2
I think what is written in ABBA blogs/communities is reliable	4,9	3,4	4,1	3,9	4,6
I think the communication in ABBA blogs/communities is free from being interfered by sales-persons	5,0	3,3	4,4	4,3	4,6
I think the communication in ABBA blogs/communities is free from being interfered by friends outside the ABBA com	4,9	3,6	4,4	4,0	4,7
My self-image fits with the identity of the community	4,1	2,3	3,0	2,6	3,9
When I'm interacting with the community my personal identity is strengthened	3,9	2,1	2,9	2,1	3,4
I am very attached to the user group	3,8	2,4	2,8	2,0	3,1
I have a strong feeling of belonging toward the user group	3,9	2,1	3,0	2,1	3,3
I am a valuable member of the group	3,9	2,4	3,1	2,1	3,0
I am an important member of the group	3,7	2,3	2,8	2,0	2,7

There are also other overlaps between involvement and identity segments and the motivation segments. The hooked independent fans who really identify with ABBA represent more than half of the fans in the get-togethers, thrill seekers and emotional junkies segments (fig. 3.13).

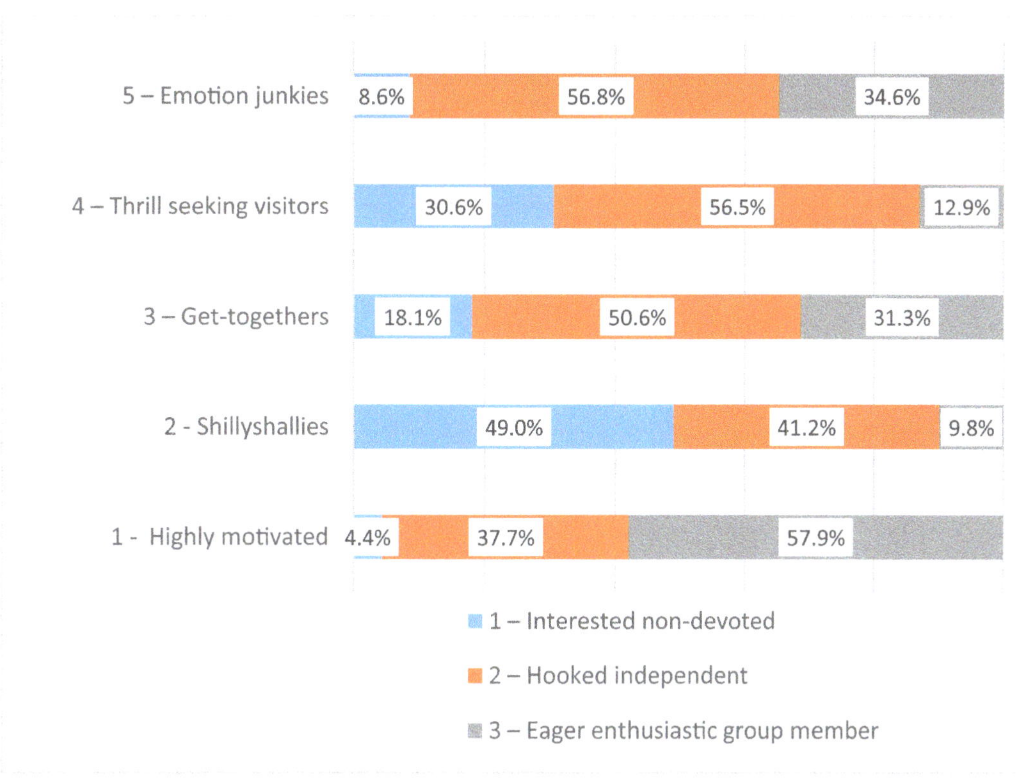

Figure 3.13. Representation of fan involvement and social identity cluster membership within motivation clusters

Emotional junkies and highly motivated fans both have high scores for offline and online fan involvement but somewhat lower scores for social identity with the community. Thrill seekers have particularly low scores for social identity and they show a lack of appreciation of ABBA online communities as an information source. The overlaps between segments also offer interesting clarity on how those who are indecisive and have low travel motivation (the shillyshallies) overlap (almost 50%) with the interested non-devoted fans who are not very involved and do not identify with the community but still consider themselves as fans. In terms of digital practices, the shillyshallies segment has the lowest scores for all aspects of offline and online fan involvement and social identity and the lowest for identification as an ABBA fan.

The highly motivated fans and get-togethers have the highest proportion of fans who attended more than 10 ABBA related trips or events (47% and 51% respectively), while thrill seeking visitors are the least experienced ABBA travelers as 32% participated in 1-2 and 49% in 3-10 ABBA related trips or events (fig. 3.14).

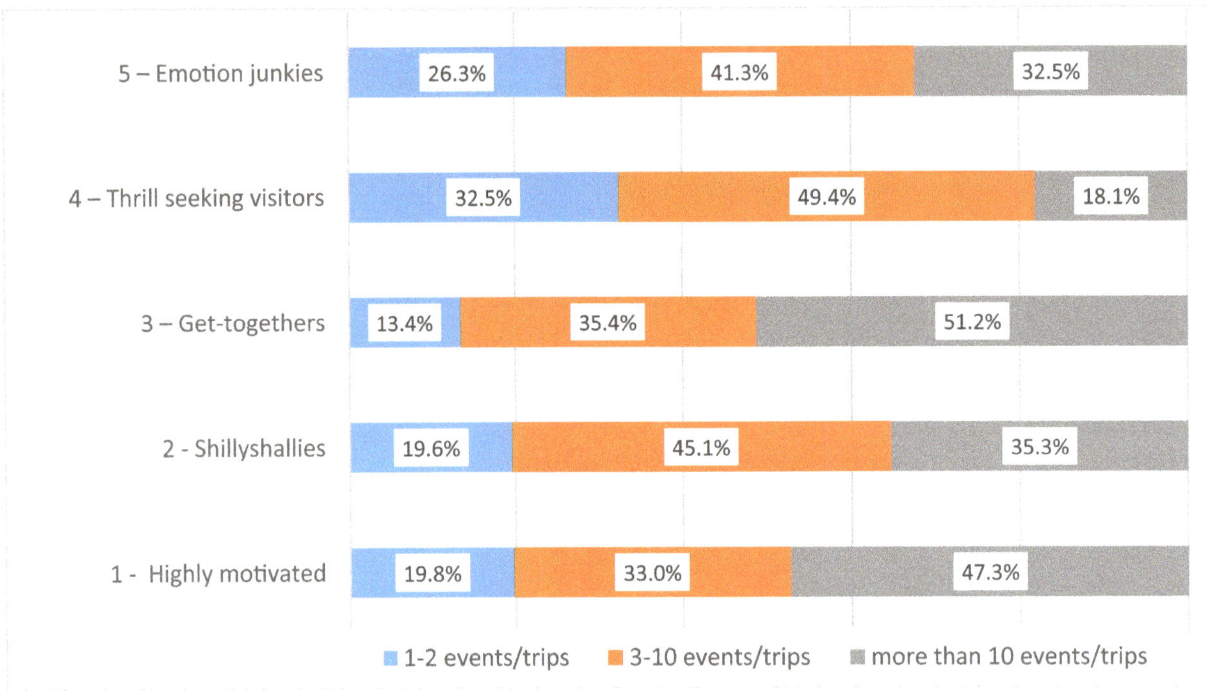

Figure 3.14. ABBA-related travel and events participation by motivation segments (sig. <0.001)

The "emotional junkies" segment has the highest proportion of solo ABBA travelers (47%) followed by "shillyshallies" (38%), while around 70% of highly motivated fans, get-togethers and thrill seekers travel with family and friends (fig. 3.15). In addition, highly motivated fans, shillyshallies and get-togethers, travel together with online friends (6-8%) more than thrill seekers and emotional junkies (1%).

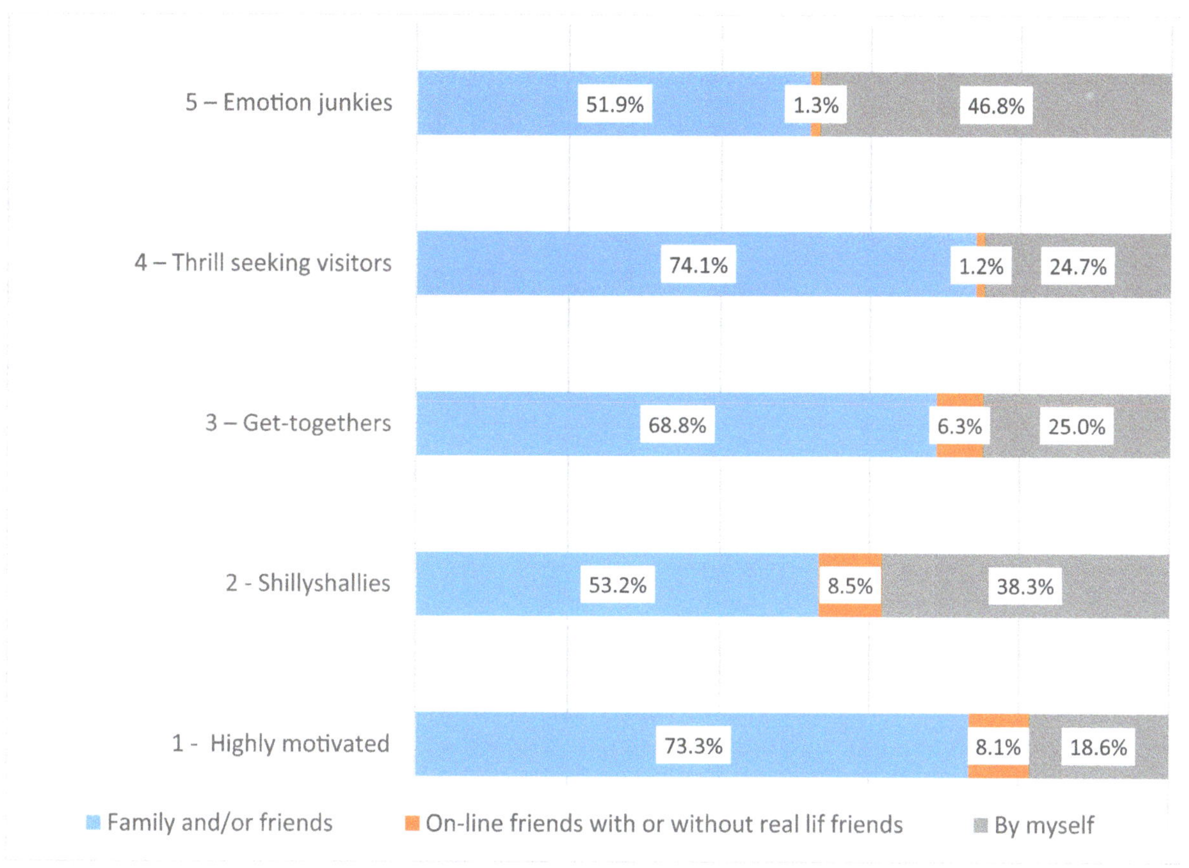

Figure 3.15. Travel accompaniment by motivation segments
(sig. <0.001)

3.4 ABBA-related web usage

The digital aspects of ABBA fans show that the vast majority of the eager-enthusiastic-group-member segment visit ABBA websites, blogs or communities very often, i.e. every day (63%) or every week (23%). The hooked independent segment is a little less active in their ABBA web usage than eager-enthusiastic fans. Nevertheless, about 70% of hooked independent fans visit ABBA-related websites, blogs or communities every day or every week. The situation is the opposite for the interested non-devoted fans, as the majority (60%) visit ABBA online resources a few times every month or less (fig. 3.16).

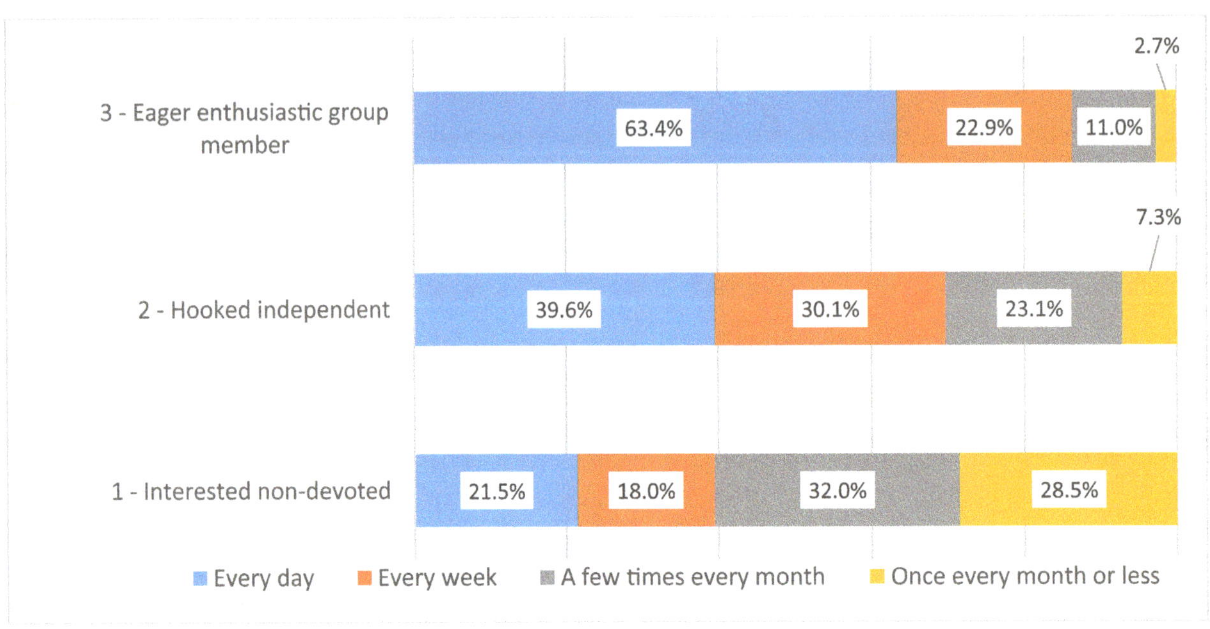

Figure 3.16. Average ABBA-related web sites visitation by fan involvement and social identity segments (sig. <0.001)

ABBA fans who visit ABBA websites, blogs or communities every day also show the highest degree of fan involvement manifested through the activity-based fan-involvement index (fig. 3.17).

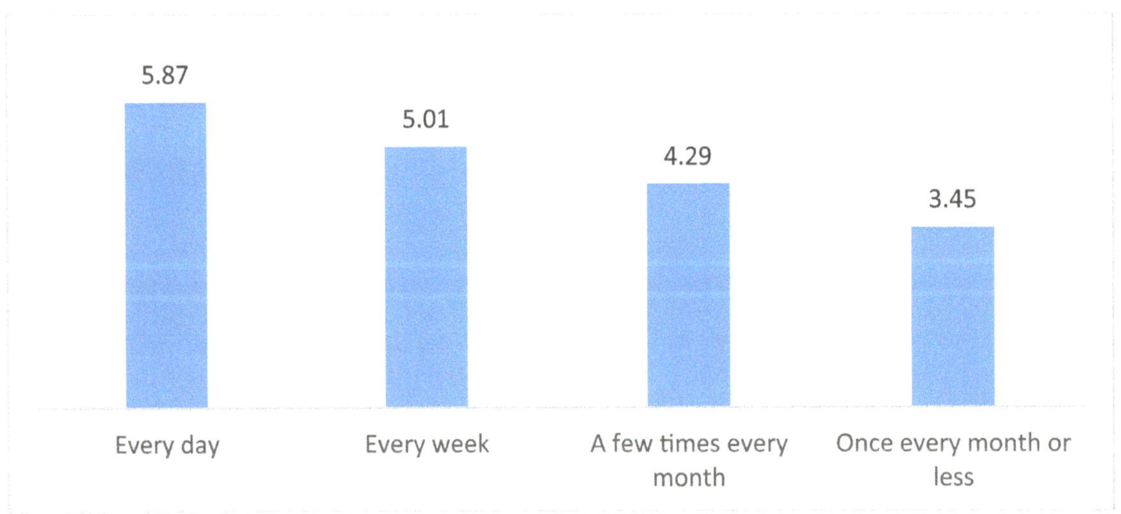

Figure 3.17. Relationship between activity-based fan involvement (fan involvement index score) and average ABBA-related website visitation frequency (sig. <0.001)

Active online fans also travel more since about half of those who visit ABBA websites, blogs or communities daily also participated in more than 10 ABBA related trips or events.

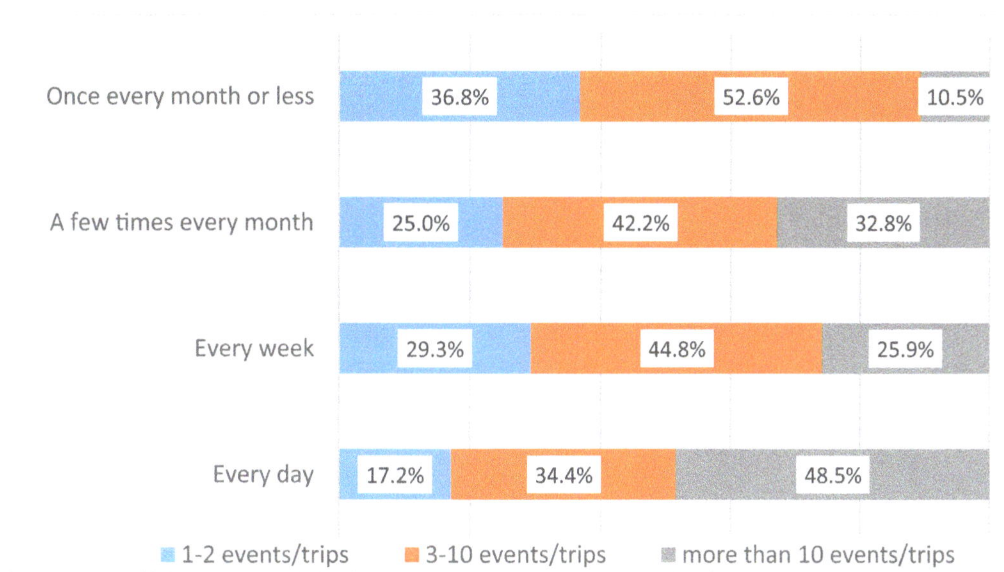

Figure 3.18. Relationship between ABBA-related website usage and participation in trips/events (sig. <0.001)

Active online fans also demonstrate the highest degree of social identity and score highest on the travel motives related to being part of an ABBA community, experiencing the ABBA atmosphere and appreciating the social aspects of ABBA travel such as partying, meeting old and new friends, and sharing experience with their travel companions (tables 3.9 and 3.10).

Table 3.9. Fan involvement and social identity based on ABBA web usage behavior 1-7), sig. <0.001

Variables	Daily	Weekly	Few times a month	Once a month or less
To what extent would you say you are an ABBA fan?	6,8	6,6	6,4	6,2
I'm interested in ABBA	6,7	6,7	6,5	6,1
I feel that ABBA is essential to me, therefore I prioritize ABBA over my other hobbies	5,5	4,7	4,1	3,1
Purchasing ABBA products is a way of rewarding myself	5,3	4,8	4,1	3,2
The ABBA products I purchase symbolize my personality and character	4,9	4,4	3,9	3,2
I'm interested in reading information and seeing photos of ABBA in blogs/communities	6,3	6,0	5,4	4,5
When reading information in blogs/communities I feel the information is appealing	5,5	5,1	4,5	4,0
When reading information in blogs/communities I feel that ABBA is relevant in my life	5,5	4,9	4,3	3,5
When reading information in blogs/communities I feel that ABBA means a lot to me	5,8	5,2	4,5	3,7
I think ABBA blogs/communities provide good efficiency in information searching	5,6	5,1	4,5	3,7
I think ABBA blogs/communities provide sufficient information	5,4	4,9	4,5	3,7
I think what is written in ABBA blogs/communities is reliable	4,8	4,4	4,0	3,6
I think the communication in ABBA blogs/communities is free from being interfered by sales-persons	4,8	4,5	4,1	3,6
I think the communication in ABBA blogs/communities is free from being interfered by friends outside the ABBA community	4,8	4,6	4,1	3,7
My self-image fits with the identity of the community	3,9	3,6	3,2	2,4
When I'm interacting with the community my personal identity is strengthened	3,7	3,2	2,9	2,1
I am very attached to the user group	3,5	2,8	2,3	1,8
I have a strong feeling of belonging toward the user group	3,7	3,0	2,5	1,8
I am a valuable member of the group	3,5	2,8	2,4	1,7
I am an important member of the group	3,3	2,6	2,3	1,6

Table 3.10. Motivation to travel and participate in ABBA-related events based on ABBA web usage behavior (1-7)

Variables	Daily	Weekly	Few times a month	Once a month or less	Sig.
To experience a sense of belonging to ABBA	5,5	4,9	4,9	4,4	**
To experience a sense of belonging to the ABBA community	5,4	4,6	4,2	3,4	***
To experience an "ABBA atmosphere"	6,1	5,7	5,5	5,6	**
To participate in activities that are fun	6,0	5,7	5,7	5,5	n.s.
To experience new and different things	5,4	5,5	5,4	5,2	n.s.
To get away from the usual routine	5,0	4,9	4,8	4,8	n.s.
To experience excitement	5,6	5,6	5,3	4,8	n.s.
To party and drink	3,5	3,2	2,8	2,4	*
To be with people who are enjoying themselves	5,1	4,7	4,4	3,8	**
To meet old friends	4,6	3,9	3,4	3,6	***
To meet new friends	4,6	3,9	3,7	3,1	***
To share the experience with the people traveling with me	5,0	4,6	4,8	3,6	*
To have fun with my friends and/or family	5,4	5,4	5,1	4,6	n.s.
To participate in other activities that are not ABBA related	4,1	4,4	4,1	4,5	n.s.
To visit an attractive destination	4,9	5,1	5,1	5,4	n.s.
To visit this particular destination	5,1	5,3	5,2	5,9	n.s.
To watch people and be a part of the event/trip	4,8	4,5	4,2	4,1	n.s.

Significance level (ANOVA): *** (<0.001), ** (<0.01), * (<0.1)

Unsurprisingly, the travel motive to interact with other fans is essential for the absolute majority of ABBA fans travelling with their online friends. The eager-enthusiastic-group-member segment and those visiting ABBA websites, blogs or communities every day also largely identify interaction with other fans as an essential travel motive (table 3.11).

Table 3.11. Travel and event participation motive to interact with other fans for travel accompaniment, involvement and identity clusters and web usage behavior (1-7)

	To party and drink	To be with people who are enjoying themselves	To meet old friends	To meet new friends
Travel accompaniment				
Family and/or friends	3,3	5,0	4,1	4,1
On-line friends with or without real life friends	4,1	5,1	5,7	5,2
By myself	3,0	4,5	4,2	4,4
Sig.	*	*	**	*
Fan involvement and social identity clusters				
1 – Interested non-devoted	2,4	3,7	3,6	3,3
2 – Hooked independent	3,2	4,7	3,8	3,8
3 – Eager enthusiastic group member	3,9	5,6	5,1	5,3
Sig.	***	***	***	***
ABBA websites usage				
Every day	3,5	5,1	4,6	4,6
Every week	3,2	4,7	3,9	3,9
A few times every month	2,8	4,4	3,4	3,7
Once every month or less	2,4	3,8	3,6	3,1
Sig.	*	**	***	***

Significance level (ANOVA): *** (<0.001), ** (<0.01), * (<0.1)

The daily online users in comparison to other fans score highest on emotional aspects of web experience such as being aroused, frenzied, excited, contented, pleased and happy, indicating the importance of emotional aspects of online fan practices (table 3.12). Frequent web users also have the highest level of general interest in ABBA, identify with ABBA and interest in the online ABBA community.

Table 3.12. Emotional web experience ("The blog/community where I found the link to this survey makes me feel..."; 1-7)

Variables	Daily	Weekly	Few times a month	Once a month or less	Sig.
Unaroused - Aroused	4,6	4,1	4,1	3,9	***
Sluggish - Frenzied	4,5	4,1	4,2	4,0	**
Calm - Excited	5,2	4,6	4,5	4,2	***
Unhappy - Happy	5,9	5,7	5,4	4,9	***
Annoyed - Pleased	5,8	5,5	5,2	4,9	***
Not contented- Contented	5,6	5,2	5,1	4,7	***

Significance level (ANOVA): *** (<0.001), ** (<0.01)

Relatively frequent web users largely use information in blogs and communities to plan their participation in ABBA-related travel. It is clear that online fan practices affect future travel intentions since the absolute majority of ABBA fans (92%) that use information in blogs and online communities for planning trips and events, agree that it also influenced their final decision. There are slight differences between the involvement and identity segments where eager-enthusiastic-group-member fans use blogs to plan their ABBA-related travel more (83%) than the hooked independent fans (62%). There is a similar difference between these segments in respect to how this influenced their travel decision. Among the interested non-devoted fans there is much less (62% state to a low extent or not at all) use of blogs or communities to plan ABBA-related travel and the information mostly (81%) did not influence their travel decision.

In respect to the motivation-based segments, highly motivated fans and get-togethers to a great extent use blogs or communities to plan ABBA-related travel and over half in each group consider blogs or communities important for their decision to travel. Use of blogs or communities to plan their travel is lowest among shillyshallies and thrill seekers even though over half of them in each group do so (figures 3.19 and 3.20).

The emotions evoked by using blogs or communities show the highest scores for the eager enthusiastic ABBA fans, highly motivated fans, fans that widely use blogs or communities for travel planning and decision-making, as well as fans with the lowest income below $20,000. The emotional junkies segment score high on excitement, happiness and pleasure when using ABBA blogs or communities. The singles group as opposed to those in a relationship have higher scores for emotional response in terms of arousal, frenzy, excitement and happiness (table 3.13).

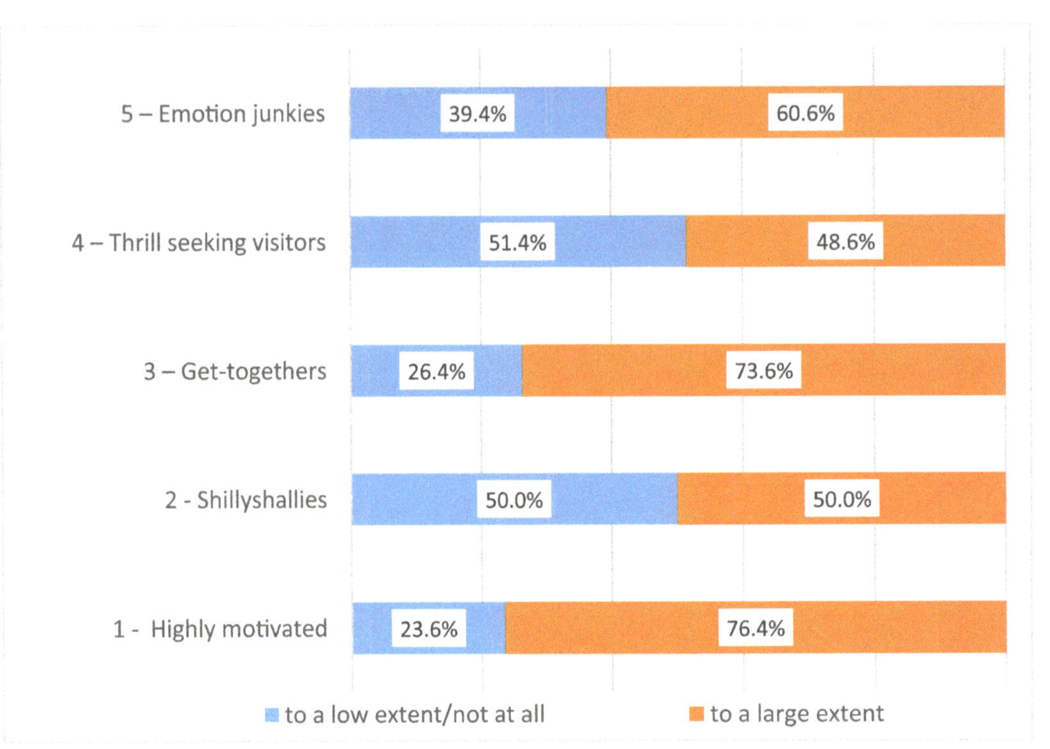

Figure 3.19. Use of information in blogs/communities to plan participation by ABBA-related trips/events by motivation segments (sig. <0.001)

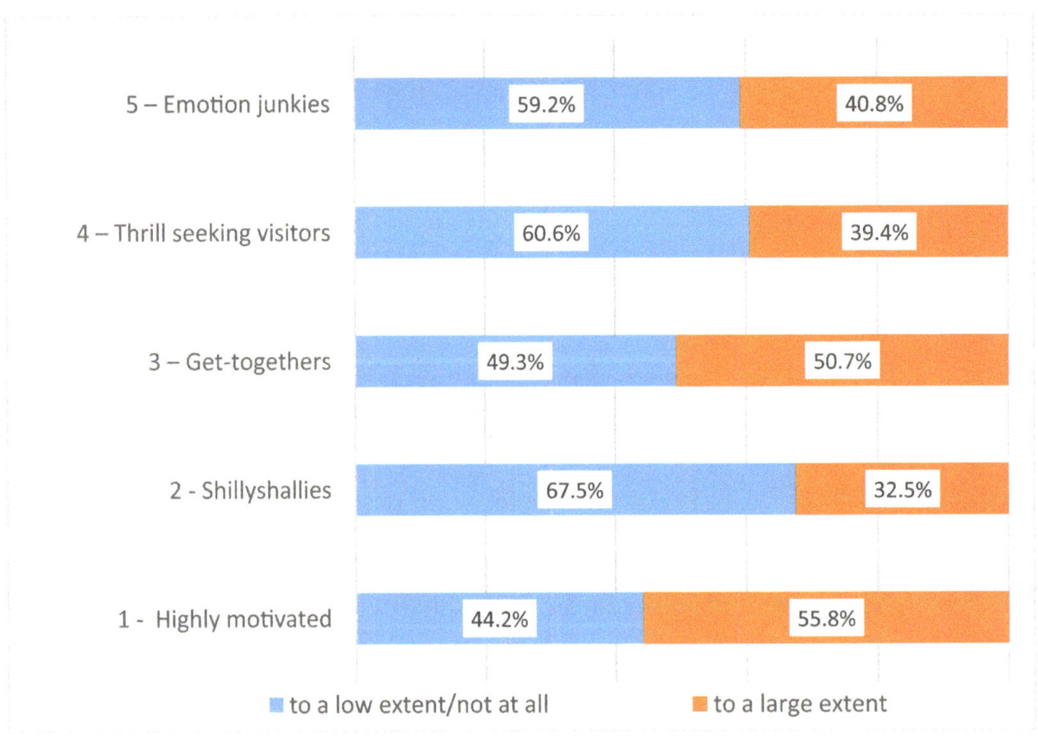

Figure 3.20. Impact of information in blogs/communities on the decision to participate by ABBA-related trips/events by motivation segments (sig. <0.05)

Table 3.13. Emotional web experience for various groups of fans

Variables	Unaroused - Aroused	Sluggish - Frenzied	Calm - Excited	Unhappy - Happy	Annoyed - Pleased	Not contented- Contented
Relationship status						
Singles	4,5	4,4	5,0	5,8	5,6	5,4
Couples	4,1	4,1	4,6	5,5	5,4	5,2
Sig.	**	*	***	*	n.s.	n.s.
Income level						
Less than $19 999	4,7	4,7	5,3	6,1	6,0	5,6
$20 000-49 999	4,4	4,3	4,7	5,7	5,5	5,4
$50 000-89 999	4,1	4,0	4,5	5,4	5,3	5,1
More than $90000	4,2	4,2	4,8	5,6	5,4	5,3
Sig.	**	***	***	***	***	*
Fan involvement and social identity clusters						
Interested non-devoted	3,5	3,5	3,7	4,7	4,7	4,4
Hooked independent	4,2	4,2	4,7	5,6	5,4	5,2
Eager enthusiastic group member	5,0	4,9	5,7	6,4	6,2	6,0
Sig.	***	***	***	***	***	***
Motivation clusters						
Highly motivated	4,8	4,7	5,4	6,1	5,9	5,7
Shillyshallies	3,8	3,8	3,9	5,3	5,4	4,9
Get togethers	4,0	3,9	4,5	5,3	5,4	5,2
Thrill seekers	3,9	4,1	4,4	5,3	5,1	5,1
Emotion junkies	4,2	4,0	5,1	6,1	5,8	5,4
Sig.	***	***	***	***	**	**

Table 3.13 (continues)

Variables	Unaroused - Aroused	Sluggish - Frenzied	Calm - Excited	Unhappy - Happy	Annoyed - Pleased	Not contented- Contented
Use of information in blogs/communities to plan participation in trips/events						
to a low extent/not at all	3,9	3,9	4,4	5,4	5,3	4,9
to a large extent	4,5	4,4	5,1	5,9	5,7	5,5
Sig.	***	*	***	*	*	***
Impact of information in blogs/communities on the decision to participate in trips/events						
low	4,1	4,1	4,7	5,6	5,4	5,1
high	4,6	4,5	5,1	5,9	5,8	5,6
Sig.	**	*	*	*	*	**

Significance level (t-tests, ANOVA): *** (<0.001), ** (<0.01), * (<0.1)

3.5 Perceived value and travel intentions

The results show that the involvement and social identity segment of eager-enthusiastic-group members have the highest scores on all aspects (functional, emotional and social) of perceived value of the ABBA related trip or event. This includes the overall quality evaluation, value for money, time and effort spent, enjoyment, excitement, escape, being absorbed by the experience, novelty value of learning about new information and trends, as well as the social value of acceptance, approval, self-esteem, making an impression on other people and social interaction (tables 3.14 and 3.15). The same applies to the highly motivated fans. The emotional junkies segment has somewhat lower scores on the novelty value and social value but high scores on other aspects perceived value. The segments with less involved and more indecisive fans (the non-devoted and shillyshallies) have the lowest scores on all aspects of perceived value (tables 3.16 and 3.17).

The daily visitors of ABBA websites and online communities experience the highest levels of excitement, accomplishment and all social value aspects and the less frequent users (i.e., once every month or less) the lowest (table 3.18). The results again demonstrate the digital aspects of fan practice in relation to travel since fans who extensively use information in blogs and online communities to plan their participation, obtain significantly higher levels of perceived value and social value (table 3.19).

The single ABBA fans experience high levels of value in terms of novelty, acceptance, approval and the value of social interaction with other people (table 3.20). In addition, fans travelling together with their online friends experience social approval more than other fans and use ABBA trips and events as an opportunity to interact and communicate with other people (table 3.21). An interesting result is that the social value scores are highest among the fans in the lowest income group (table 3.22). Finally, expenditures for the trip or event does not impact perceived value and social value with the only exception of novelty, as the fans with the highest total expenditures above $1,000 use the ABBA-related trip or event to learn about new information and trends (5.1 compared to 4.1-4.4 for fans with lower expenditures levels, sig. <0.01).

The results indicate how involved, motivated, online active and experienced fans are significantly more inclined to participate in ABBA trips and events in the future and to recommend others to do so (tables 3.23-3.26). It is also evident that fans that are emotionally and socially motivated (emotional junkies and get-togethers) are also quite positive regarding their future intentions and willingness to recommend ABBA trips and events to others. The eager-enthusiastic-group-members, the highly motivated fans and the relatively frequent (at least weekly) users of online platforms as well as those who use online information to plan their trip or event participation, actually share their experiences on blogs and communities more than others (tables 3.23-3.25, figure 3.21).

Table 3.14. Perceived value of ABBA related trip or event by fan involvement and social identity segments (sig. <0.001)

Variable	Interested non-devoted	Hooked independent	Eager enthusiastic group member
The event/trip had a consistent quality	5,3	5,7	6,2
Relative to other events/trips I have participated at, this event/trip had an acceptable level of quality	5,3	5,6	6,2
The event/trip was as expected	5,3	5,7	6,0
The event/trip exceeded my expectations	4,8	5,4	5,7
The event/trip was a good purchase for the price paid	5,2	5,7	6,1
The event/trip was reasonably priced	4,8	5,4	5,8
The event/trip was well worth the time and effort spent	5,5	6,0	6,4
The price was the main criterion for the decision to participate	2,7	3,1	3,8
By participating at an ABBA related event/trip I acccomplished just what I need	4,0	5,5	5,9
I am comfortable with the event/trip I purchased	5,3	5,9	6,4
I enjoyed the event/trip	5,9	6,3	6,6
The event/trip made me feel good	5,8	6,3	6,7
During the event/trip I felt absorbed by the experience	4,6	5,7	6,2
The event/trip was an escape	3,3	4,2	5,1
The event/trip gave me a chance to learn about new information and trends	3,2	4,3	4,9
The event/trip made me excited	4,6	5,8	6,4
Compared to other things I could have done, the time and effort spent on this event/trip was truly enjoyable	5,5	6,1	6,5

Table 3.15. Social value of ABBA related trip or event by fan involvement and social identity segments (sig. <0.001)

Variable	Interested non-devoted	Hooked independent	Eager enthusiastic group member
Participating at this event/trip helped me to feel acceptable	2,2	3,2	4,6
This type of event/trip is taken by many people I know	2,9	3,5	5,0
Participating at this event/trip improved the way I am perceived by others	2,0	2,7	4,2
People who participate at this type of event/trip obtain social approval	1,9	2,7	4,0
I participated at this event/trip to make a good impression on other people	1,6	2,0	2,9
I participated at this event/trip to be able to interact and communicate with other people	2,8	3,5	5,0

Table 3.16. Perceived value of ABBA related trip or event by motivation segments (sig. <0.001)

Variable	Highly motivated	Shilly-shallies	Get togethers	Thrill seekers	Emotion junkies
The event/trip had a consistent quality	6,4	4,1	5,3	5,9	6,0
Relative to other events/trips I have participated at, this event/trip had an acceptable level of quality	6,3	4,2	5,4	5,8	5,7
The event/trip was as expected	6,3	4,4	5,4	5,8	5,7
The event/trip exceeded my expectations	6,1	3,4	4,9	5,4	5,6
The event/trip was a good purchase for the price paid	6,4	4,0	5,5	5,8	5,8
The event/trip was reasonably priced	6,0	4,1	5,1	5,4	5,6
The event/trip was well worth the time and effort spent	6,5	4,5	5,8	6,1	6,1
The price was the main criterion for the decision to participate	4,0	2,5	3,0	2,7	3,1
By participating at an ABBA related event/trip I acccomplished just what I need	6,1	3,7	4,9	4,9	5,9
I am comfortable with the event/trip I purchased	6,5	4,3	5,6	6,1	6,2
I enjoyed the event/trip	6,8	4,8	6,2	6,5	6,4
The event/trip made me feel good	6,8	4,7	6,1	6,5	6,4
During the event/trip I felt absorbed by the experience	6,4	3,7	5,1	5,6	6,1
The event/trip was an escape	5,3	2,4	3,9	3,8	4,7
The event/trip gave me a chance to learn about new information and trends	5,2	2,6	3,7	4,2	4,2
The event/trip made me excited	6,5	3,8	5,2	5,8	6,1
Compared to other things I could have done, the time and effort spent on this event/trip was truly enjoyable	6,7	4,4	5,8	6,1	6,4

Table 3.17. Social value of ABBA related trip or event by motivation segments (sig. <0.001)

Variable	Highly motivated	Shilly-shallies	Get togethers	Thrill seekers	Emotion junkies
Participating at this event/trip helped me to feel acceptable	4,4	2,0	3,3	2,5	3,7
This type of event/trip is taken by many people I know	5,1	2,4	4,5	2,4	3,3
Participating at this event/trip improved the way I am perceived by others	4,1	1,9	2,9	2,2	2,7
People who participate at this type of event/trip obtain social approval	3,9	1,8	2,8	2,3	2,8
I participated at this event/trip to make a good impression on other people	2,8	1,9	2,1	1,8	1,8
I participated at this event/trip to be able to interact and communicate with other people	5,2	2,7	3,8	2,8	3,0

Table 3.18. Perceived and social value of ABBA related trip or event by website usage categories of ABBA fans

Variable	Daily	Weekly	A few times every month	Once every month or less	Sig.
Perceived value					
By participating at an ABBA related event/trip I accomplished just what I need	5,6	5,2	5,0	5,0	*
The event/trip made me excited	5,9	5,8	5,5	4,9	*
Social value					
Participating at this event/trip helped me to feel acceptable	3,8	3,3	3,2	2,5	**
This type of event/trip is taken by many people I know	4,4	3,4	3,2	2,8	***
Participating at this event/trip improved the way I am perceived by others	3,4	2,8	2,7	2,0	***
People who participate at this type of event/trip obtain social approval	3,3	2,7	2,5	2,3	***
I participated at this event/trip to make a good impression on other people	2,4	2,1	1,8	1,5	*
I participated at this event/trip to be able to interact and communicate with other people	4,2	3,5	3,6	2,7	***

Significance level (ANOVA): *** (<0.001), ** (<0.01), * (<0.1)

Table 3.19. Perceived and social value of ABBA related trip or event by ABBA fans using information in blogs/communities to plan participation

Variable	to a low extent/not at all	to a large extent	Sig.
Perceived value			
Relative to other events/trips I have participated at, this event/trip had an acceptable level of quality	5,3	6,0	***
The event/trip was as expected	5,5	5,9	**
The event/trip exceeded my expectations	4,9	5,6	***
The event/trip was a good purchase for the price paid	5,5	5,9	**
The event/trip was reasonably priced	5,2	5,6	*
The event/trip was well worth the time and effort spent	5,7	6,3	***
The price was the main criterion for the decision to participate	2,9	3,4	*
By participating at an ABBA related event/trip I acccomplished just what I need	5,0	5,6	***

I am comfortable with the event/trip I purchased	5,7	6,2	***
I enjoyed the event/trip	6,0	6,6	***
The event/trip made me feel good	6,1	6,5	***
During the event/trip I felt absorbed by the experience	5,3	6,0	***
The event/trip was an escape	3,8	4,7	***
The event/trip gave me a chance to learn about new information and trends	3,9	4,6	**
The event/trip made me excited	5,5	6,0	**
Compared to other things I could have done, the time and effort spent on this event/trip was truly enjoyable	5,8	6,3	***
Social value			
Participating at this event/trip helped me to feel acceptable	2,8	3,8	***
This type of event/trip is taken by many people I know	3,0	4,4	***
Participating at this event/trip improved the way I am perceived by others	2,4	3,4	***
People who participate at this type of event/trip obtain social approval	2,4	3,3	***
I participated at this event/trip to make a good impression on other people	1,9	2,3	*
I participated at this event/trip to be able to interact and communicate with other people	3,2	4,2	***

Significance level (t-test): *** (<0.001), ** (<0.01), * (<0.1)

Table 3.20. Perceived and social value of ABBA related trip or event by ABBA fans with different relationship status

	Single with or without children	Married/Common law husband/wife with or without children	Sig.
Perceived value			
The event/trip gave me a chance to learn about new information and trends	4,6	4,1	*
Social value			
Participating at this event/trip helped me to feel acceptable	3,8	3,3	*
Participating at this event/trip improved the way I am perceived by others	3,5	2,9	**
People who participate at this type of event/trip obtain social approval	3,4	2,8	**
I participated at this event/trip to be able to interact and communicate with other people	4,4	3,7	**

Significance level (t-test): *** (<0.001), ** (<0.01), * (<0.1)

Table 3.21. Social value of ABBA related trip or event by travel accompaniment

	Family and/or friends	On-line friends with or without real life friends	By myself	Sig.
This type of event/trip is taken by many people I know	3,9	5,4	3,7	***
Participating at this event/trip improved the way I am perceived by others	3,1	4,0	2,9	*
I participated at this event/trip to make a good impression on other people	2,3	2,9	2,0	*
I participated at this event/trip to be able to interact and communicate with other people	3,8	5,1	3,9	*

Significance level (t-test): *** (<0.001), ** (<0.01), * (<0.1)

Table 3.22. Social value of ABBA related trip or event by income group

	< $19 999	$20 000-49 999	$50 000-89 999	> $90000	Sig.
Participating at this event/trip helped me to feel acceptable	4,3	3,5	3,7	3,1	*
This type of event/trip is taken by many people I know	4,7	4,2	3,8	3,6	**
Participating at this event/trip improved the way I am perceived by others	3,7	3,4	3,1	2,7	**
People who participate at this type of event/trip obtain social approval	3,6	3,2	2,9	2,8	*
I participated at this event/trip to be able to interact and communicate with other people	4,6	4,3	3,9	3,5	**

Significance level (t-test): *** (<0.001), ** (<0.01), * (<0.1)

Table 3.23. Comparison of future behavior intentions, willingness to recommend and electronic word-of-mouth based on fan identity and involvement cluster membership, (1-7), sig. <0.001

	Interested non-devoted	Hooked independent	Eager enthusiastic group member
Willingness to participate at an ABBA related event/trip	4,0	5,6	6,4
Willingness to recommend others to participate at an ABBA related event/trip	3,6	5,0	6,2
After I participated, I have shared my experiences on blogs/communities	2,9	3,8	5,1

Table 3.24. Comparison of future behavior intentions, willingness to recommend and electronic word-of-mouth based on motivation cluster membership (1-7), sig. <0.001

	Highly motivated	A-bit-of-everything (fluids/shilly shally)	Get-togethers	Thrill seeking visitors	Social emotional spirits (emotion junkies)
Willingness to participate at an ABBA related event/trip	6,8	5,2	6,1	5,8	6,4
Willingness to recommend others to participate at an ABBA related event/trip	6,6	3,9	5,7	4,8	5,8
After I participated, I have shared my experiences on blogs/communities	4,9	2,9	4,1	3,3	4,2

Table 3.25. Comparison of future behavior intentions, willingness to recommend and electronic word-of-mouth based on ABBA websites usage (1-7), sig. <0.001

	Every day	Every week	A few times every month	Once every month or less
Willingness to participate at an ABBA related event/trip	5,9	5,6	5,1	3,9
Willingness to recommend others to participate at an ABBA related event/trip	5,6	5,2	4,7	3,6
After I participated, I have shared my experiences on blogs/communities	4,6	3,8	3,4	2,0

Table 3.26. Comparison of future behavior intentions and willingness to recommend based on ABBA-related travel and event participation experience (1-7), sig. <0.001

	1-2 events/trips	3-10 events/trips	more than 10 events/trips
Willingness to participate at an ABBA related event/trip	6,1	6,0	6,5
Willingness to recommend others to participate at an ABBA related event/trip	5,5	5,3	6,1

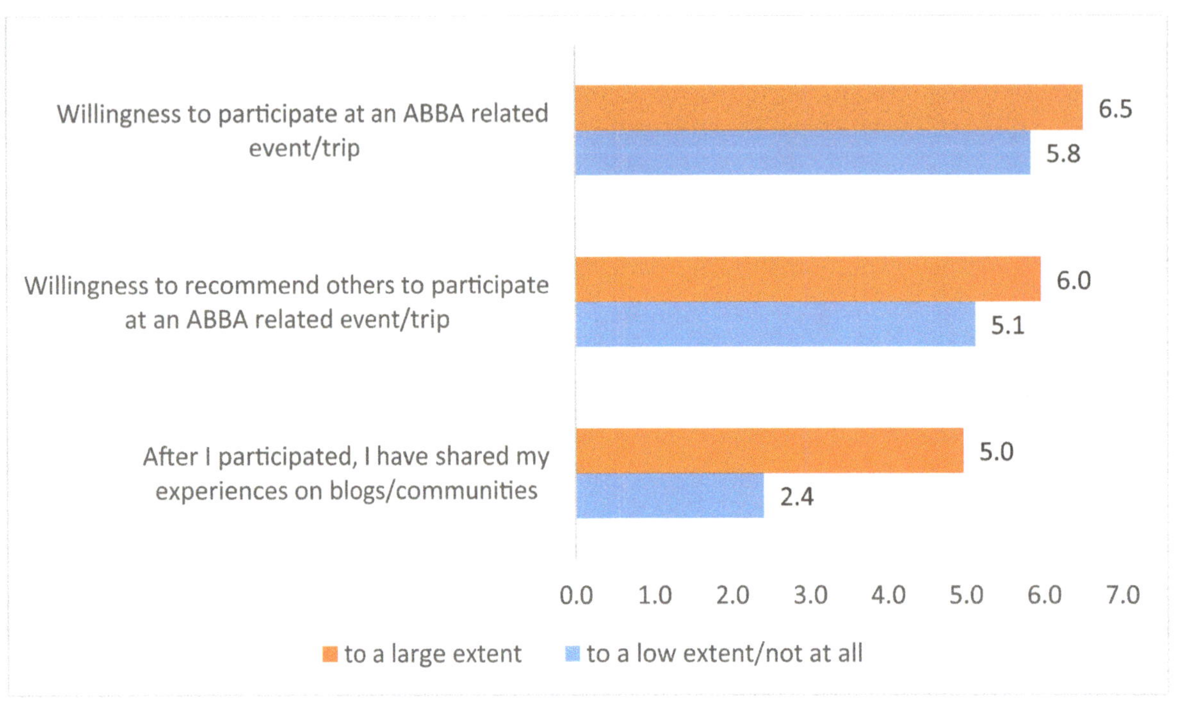

Figure 3.21. Electronic word-of-mouth based on the degree of using the ABBA-related information to plan participation in ABBA-related trips and events, sig.<0.001

4 Model testing

This study uses a structural equation modelling approach for testing the relationships between the concepts described in the previous section. In total, the subset of 373 cases was available for model testing (i.e., the respondents provided at least one answer per each construct in the model; the missing values were substituted by means). Furthermore, z-score-examination revealed outliers ($z>3.29$) being substituted with "the next highest score plus one" (Field, 2005, p. 116).

The step of confirmatory factor analysis (CFA) performed by using the AMOS (ver. 24) software package started by examination of the unidimensionality of the specified model measurement. All unstandardized loadings (i.e., regression weights) were statistically different from zero. All t-values were higher than 1.96. However, considering that the overall model-fit-statistics measures were somewhat below recommended thresholds (Brown, 2006), the measurement model adjustment was required.

Examination of standardized loadings (i.e. < 0.50), standardized residuals (i.e. > 2.58) and modification indices resulted in the removal of 11 out of 63 items intended for model measurement (one motive item, three online fan involvement items, two social identity items, three preceived value and two social value items). Table 4.1. shows the goodness of fit statistics for the adjusted model, which remain somewhat below but close to the recommended threshold values (Steenkamp & Baumgartner, 2000; Hair et al., 2010).

Table 4.1. CFA goodness-of-fit statistics

Indicator [Threshold value]	Statistic value
Absolute Fit Measures	
Goodness-of-fit Index (GFI) [>0.90]	0.773
Root Mean Square Error of Approximation (RMSEA) [<0.08: acceptable fit; < 0.05: good fit]	0.061
90 percent confidence interval for RMSEA [0.05;0.08]	(0.058; 0.065)
Normed-Chi-Square ($\chi2/df$) [<2]	2425.516/1009=2.404
Incremental Fit Indices	
Tucker-Lewis Index (TLI) [>0.90]	0.87

Comparative Fit Index (CFI) [>0.90]	0.87
Parsimony Fit Indices	
Adjusted Goodness-of-fit Index (AGFI) [>0.80]	0.75

After transformation of the measurement model into a structural model a linear structural equation model (SEM) using maximum likelihood (ML) estimation is applied to test the hypothesised relationships between the model constructs (Hair et al., 2010). Figure 5.1 displays the path diagram and shows standardized estimates and squared multiple correlations (R^2).

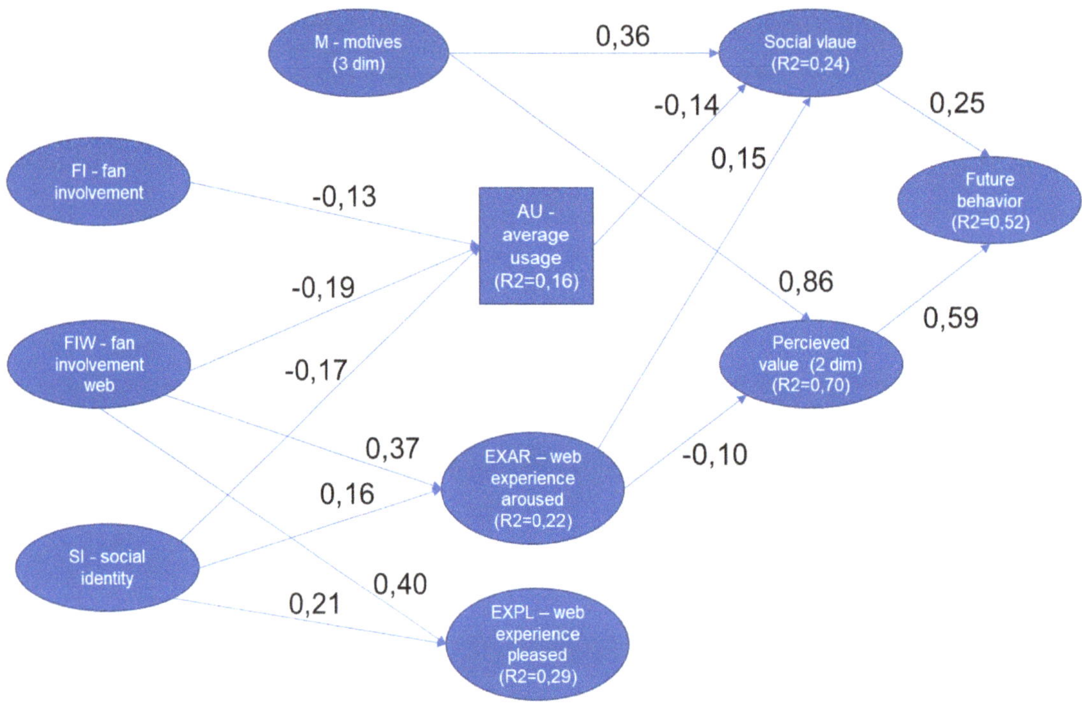

Figure 4.1. Standardized path estimates for the structural model

Overall, the level of involvement among fans, fans perceived association with the ABBA community and their interest in and perception of information in blogs and online communities, affects their average use of online platforms. This, in turn, has a modest positive effect on social value implying that when fans prioritize their interest and sense that ABBA products are rewarding and closely tied to their personality, they engage online more frequently. They also engage more when they are generally very interested as well as believing it is an efficient way of finding information. When their self-image fits with the community or they have a strong feeling of belonging, attachment and membership (social identity), they also engage more frequently online, which then results in a positive social value (i.e. a sense of social approval, self-esteem and positive perception and acceptance by others).

Furthermore, the positive effect of online engagement on excitement and feeling pleased when online as well as for social value and future intentions, is evidence of how digital interactions influence perceptions of value and future intentions. When fans have a great interest in blogs and communities and find them appealing, personally meaningful, reliable, offering an efficient way of finding information, and is free from commercial interests, then they feel happy, pleased and contented but also aroused, frenzied and excited. This in turn supports their social value in terms of feeling of acceptance, approval, self-esteem and impression on other people and eventually affects the likelihood to travel or to recommend others.

It is interesting to note however, that social identity (attachment, belongingness, membership and sense of fit between self-image and identity of the community), is less important for creating positive web experiences and increased likelihood of future ABBA related travel.

As expected from previous tourism literature, travel motives have considerable importance for perceived experience value (Prebensen, Woo, Chen and Uysal). However, some of the typical motives for travel such as meeting friends and partying are of less importance for attaining high levels of functional, emotional and social value compared to those involving excitement, experiencing new and different things as well as a bond to ABBA and the ABBA community. In turn, future travel intentions depend very much on perceived emotional, social and functional value. Especially, fans who experience feelings of absorption, escape, excitement and learning new things are more interested in ABBA related travel in the future. Elements of perceived value such as high quality experiences, meeting expectations, value for money, enjoyment, and that the trip was worth the time and effort are also important for establishing an interest in future travel.

5 References

Dholakia, U. M., Bagozzi, R. P., & Klein Pearo, L. (2004). A social influence model of consumer participation in network- and small-group.-based virtual communities, *International Journal of Research in Marketing, 21*, 241-263.

Cheung, C. M. K., & Lee, M. K. O. (2010). A theoretical model of intentional social action in online social networks. *Decision Support Systems, 49*, 24-30.

Coan, James A. & Allen, John, J. B. (2007). *Handbook of emotion elicitation and assessment.* Oxford, New York: Oxford University Press.

Huang, C.Y., Chou, C.J., & Lin, P.C. (2010). Involvement theory in constructing bloggers' intention to purchase travel products. *Tourism Management, 31*, 513-526.

Prebensen, N. K., Woo, E., Chen, J. S., & Uysal, M. (2013). Motivation and involvement as antecedents of the perceived value of the destination experience. *Journal of travel research, 52(2)*, 253-264.

Brown, T.A. (2006). *Confirmatory Factor Analysis for Applied Research.* New York, London: The Guilford Press.

Field, A. (2005). *Discovering statistics using SPSS.* SAGE Publications.

Hair, J.F. Jr., Black, W.C., Babin, B.J., & Anderson, R.E. (2010). *Multivariate Data Analysis. A Global Perspective.* 7th ed. Pearson.

Steenkamp, J.-B.E.M., & H. Baumgartner (2000). On the Use of Structural Equation Models for Marketing Modelling. *International Journal of Research in Marketing, 17(2)*, 195-202.

Acknowledgments

I'd like to thank the many people who were kind enough to be interviewed for this book. They include Mike Watson, Janne Schaffer, and Finn Sjoberg, who played with ABBA; Ludvig Andersson, Carl Magnus Palm, Maria Lexhagen, Martha Banta, Jessica Klingberg, Calle Norlen, Gareth Owen, Stany Van Wymeersh, Helga Van de Kar, Victoria Norback, Jared Raab, John Semley, Ola Johansson, Tracey Beck, Kevin Williams, and Sandra Miller Kinge.

And, of course, I'd like to thank ABBA for the pure joy they've brought to so many people around the world with their music.

About the Author

Michael Mascioni has written extensively on music, entertainment, and interactive media/immersive media.

He was co-author of "The Out-of-Home Immersive Entertainment Frontier." He also wrote a chapter on the future of immersive media in amusement parks for "50:50 – Scenarios for the Next 50 Years" and a chapter on the future of ambient interactivity in public places for "FutureScapes – The Future of Business."

He wrote "New Startup and Innovation Models in Government and Politics" and "Reinventing Government Through Political Entrepreneurship and Exponential Innovation."

Mr. Mascioni writes freelance for such publications as Rock Cellar magazine, XS Rock, Innovation & Tech Today, and Hotelier. He was managing editor of the A&A Monthly Newsletter on Interactive Entertainment.

Mr. Mascioni holds a B.A. in English from St. Lawrence University and an M.S. in Management from the Polytechnic Institute of NY (now Poly/NYU).

Michael Mascioni is a conference planner and futurist focusing on digital media, technology, and innovation.

He was co-chairman of the Future of Immersive Leisure conferences, which focused on the use of immersive media in amusement parks, museums, and other leisure facilities. He was also the Program Director of the Intertainment Conferences on Interactive Entertainment.